T0209374

Anything Matches If You Wear It with Confidence

Natalie Merrill

WESTBOW
PRESS®
A DIVISION OF THOMAS NELSON
& ZONDERVAN

This book is a work of nonfiction. Unless otherwise noted, the author
and the publisher make no explicit guarantees as to the accuracy of
the information contained in this book, and in some cases, names of
people and places have been altered to protect their privacy.

WestBow Press books may be ordered through booksellers or by contacting:

WestBow Press
A Division of Thomas Nelson & Zondervan
1663 Liberty Drive
Bloomington, IN 47403
www.westbowpress.com
1 (866) 928-1240

Because of the dynamic nature of the Internet, any web addresses or
links contained in this book may have changed since publication and
may no longer be valid. The views expressed in this work are solely those
of the author and do not necessarily reflect the views of the publisher,
and the publisher hereby disclaims any responsibility for them.

ISBN: 978-1-9736-8602-6 (sc)
ISBN: 978-1-9736-8603-3 (e)

Print information available on the last page.

WestBow Press rev. date: 3/3/2020

Contents

SECTION 3
YOU MATTER

SECTION 4
DON'T LET FEAR HOLD YOU BACK

Preface

Ever since I was a little girl, I've been fascinated with love. I'm a fan of the stereotypical romantic comedy in which the guy and the girl end up together in the end, and there is usually some dramatic declaration of love followed by a kiss you only wish would happen to you.

So that's what I spent many years doing: wishing. I wished for a first kiss in a gazebo (didn't happen), I wished for a boyfriend all throughout high school and college and my 20s (didn't happen—and still hasn't), I wished for romcoms and love songs to become realities in my life (they're not), and I've wished my whole life for love to come my way (hasn't been in the cards yet). I actually never even went on what I considered to be a real date until I was in my 30s.

I can't tell you how many times I've sat around and thought that there must be something wrong with me—that maybe there's something about me that needs to change in order for guys to be attracted to me. My friends, if you've ever thought the same thing about yourself, please know that it's just a lie in your head that isn't true. You should never have to change the unique things that make you *you* in order for someone to be drawn to you.

It took years of heartache and suppressed tears for me to realize that being me is the only person I can be. If that makes a guy scared or not interested, then he simply isn't the guy for me—end of story. I'm not going to stop listening to Taylor Swift more than any other artist; I'm not going to stop putting ketchup on everything or busting out my bag of Wheat Thins at every meal; I'm not going to stop calling my mom every day after work, no matter how old I am; I'm not going to stop sending GIFs and emojis any chance I can in text messages; I'm not going to stop posting on my blog or adjusting the content because of what one person might think; I'm not going to stop wearing the things that make me comfortable, even if other people might argue that some of my garments don't "match" (read the title of this book for my opinion on matching); and I'm not going to stop being me in any way.

You were created as you are for a purpose, and you shouldn't have to try to be someone else for anyone else. It would be wonderful if everyone could be comfortable in his or her own skin without feeling self-conscious about what other people might think. At the end of the day, who really cares?

One thing I've learned repeatedly throughout my life is that it's so important to be *you*—and to be completely OK with that. If there are self-improvements you need to make, then by all means, do so. But don't try to hide who you are because you think it might please other people—even if they're other people you really want to impress. If they don't appreciate the individual you are, then maybe they aren't worth impressing after all.

Be confident in yourself. When you learn to do that, you're able to do so many of the brave things you may have never thought possible. You can share the feelings in your heart with the person you love, you can move to a new city all by yourself where you know absolutely no one, you can quit your job that you don't like and pursue your true passion, you can boldly follow the path you know you're meant to follow, you can go to a movie or eat in a restaurant by yourself, you can take risks you were always afraid to take, and you can throw together a bunch of different pieces of your wardrobe and end up with a really great outfit that you're happy you're wearing.

Because anything matches if you wear it with confidence.

SECTION 1

YOU WERE ALWAYS MEANT TO BE YOU

When That Worry-Free
Kid Stage Ends

I adore little kids. There's something about childhood that is truly magical, and I don't mean in the Santa-can-fit-down-the-chimney and the-tooth-fairy-leaves-money-under-your-pillow kind of way. I mean in the sense that you don't really care about people's perceptions of you. You might dress yourself in a way that's comical to other people, but it's perfect to you. You aren't necessarily afraid to speak what's on your mind, and it's a lot easier to believe that you can do anything and become anything you want to be. It's as if nothing and no one can stop you from chasing down all of the dreams you have in your beautifully innocent heart.

As a kid, I was very athletic and excelled in sports. I always felt confident in my abilities as an athlete and knew that when I had that soccer ball at my feet or that basketball in my hands, I was going to score—no question about it.

I was also very much a tomboy and followed my older brother around everywhere. I wanted to play street hockey and front-yard football with him and all of his friends, regardless of how welcomed any of them made me feel. I simply showed up and did my best to show them up.

I don't know how, and I don't know why, but somewhere along

the way, that don't-mess-with-me-or-try-to-tell-me-I'm-not-good-enough attitude started to diminish a bit. I do know that it wasn't because of sports, though. If I'm being perfectly honest, I truly believe that it came as a result of me thinking that, in general, I was not good enough.

Let's start with boys and them not liking me. It seems like it always comes back to that. Here's the truth: I wasn't one of the pretty girls in school. My curly frizzy hair was the opposite of perfect, and to this day, I still don't know how to apply makeup. I can barely use my tube of lip gloss correctly. Needless to say, the fellas were never knocking on my door. I always had unreturned crushes that I only allowed to happen from afar out of fear that any guy who knew my true feelings would flee in the other direction after laughing hysterically and gagging more than a little bit. (I'm not dramatic.)

Picture, if you will, a sixth-grade girl standing in the gym at a middle school dance. Yes, it's just as awkward as you imagine. There I was with my best friend, who had just broken up with her boyfriend, which meant that pretty much every guy in the room wanted to dance with her (she was definitely one of the pretty girls). One of the guys who asked her to dance was good friends with one of the cutest guys in our grade, and basically every girl who could breathe air (including me) had a crush on him. My friend told the guy after her affections that if he wanted to dance with her, his friend needed to dance with me.

Now picture that same awkward sixth-grade girl watching the dreamy boy literally (and I do mean *literally*) being dragged across the gym floor by his friend to be forced to dance with a girl with whom he clearly didn't want to spend any time during a slow song. It hurts my stomach even now to think about it. This thought immediately rushed into my poor little tween mind: *I'm too ugly.*

And I let this belief become something I saw as a truth in my life—I was not pretty, and no guy I had feelings for would ever be interested in me.

I wish that I could hug that girl and tell her to hold on to her innocent heart but also to value the beauty she is—to know that she doesn't need to look like a Victoria's Secret model (we were all blessed in different ways) to be declared a stunning creature. She is precious and adored, and she is stronger and more capable than she will ever know. I wish that I could tell her to stop doubting herself and to go out there and take chances instead of sitting on the sidelines, too afraid to jump in the game and make the big plays.

But, unfortunately, that girl wasn't embraced by that comforting hug or those words of affirmation. Instead, I let more discouraging words fill my head. I began to become more and more insecure around guys, especially if I was attracted to them. It's like I lost all abilities to function around them. I honestly don't like admitting this, but I didn't think I was worthy enough to be seen as anything more than a fellow classmate or maybe a friend. I let myself buy the lies that there were too many things wrong with me and that I wasn't the type of girl who would ever be pursued by the guys I wanted to pursue me.

This lack of confidence started to trickle into other areas of my life, too. As a freshman in high school, I found myself less self-assured when I dribbled that basketball, and I wasn't willing to take the same risky shots I always had in the past. Even my 15 years of playing soccer seemed to be something I forgot about when I decided to join the team during my junior year. Sports were my thing—*what was happening to me?*

What was happening was that, while I was very confident in who I was as a person, I still believed that I was never going to be good enough—if I wasn't good enough to be loved by someone, why would I be worth anything in the other areas of my life?

These lies only grew as I entered high school and then college and then even into my early 20s. I went through all of high school as the single girl and watched my friends have their first boyfriends and then some. In college, my friends began entering into more serious relationships and determining if the men in their lives were their future husbands. After college, I was asked to be a bridesmaid more times than I could count (just kidding—I've been in 19 weddings, so it's clearly a countable number) and saw most of my friends start new chapters in their lives that didn't exactly include this single young woman who still hadn't had a boyfriend or even gone on a real date.

It was easy to feel sorry for myself during those times. *Why wasn't I the one falling in love? Why wasn't I the one having someone perfect for me falling in love with me?* I've watched enough romcoms to know how the story ends, and none of the situations that I'd faced was lining up. What gives, Hollywood?

Through all of those years, sadly, there was that persistent voice: *That's never going to be you. You're still not pretty enough. No guy wants a girl who looks like you.*

Oh, dear friends, pleasePLEASEpleasePLEASE don't ever get into this mindset. It's so horrible to be in a place in which you feel like you aren't enough. It's a complete and destructive lie. I look back at those years now and feel like I wasted so many opportunities just because I was too afraid of failing to overcome the not-good-enough status. Am I perfect now? Faaaarrrrr from it. But I know who I am, and I know Whose I am. I'm confident that I'm loved and enough just as I am, even in those moments when I feel lonely and forever single. I don't need someone else to complete me, and I don't need someone else's approval or acceptance of me to validate my value and worth.

And neither do you.

I do have a little bit of good news (for me, anyway): I played basketball with the guys at a company that I worked for in Dallas when I was in my early 30s, and my confidence on the court has definitely returned to its full capacity. I even took some shots that might have been better-suited for the circus.

We're not meant to be pansies in life—I like to leave that job to those ugly flowers (I hate flowers, and I'm not sorry about it). And sometimes being bold means picking up that basketball and telling yourself that you're ready for a one-on-one game with LeBron James, and you're at least pretty sure that you're going to beat him.

It's fine if you lose—at least you believed in yourself enough to try.

2

Because Getting Detention on Purpose Is Silly

I know that not everything can be as ideal as we would prefer for it to be. That's simply life. At the same time, though, it can be truly difficult to accept reality when it goes absolutely nothing like we ever hoped or imagined it would go.

I can tell you right now that I didn't sit in my room as a young girl and then as a teenager wishing and hoping to grow up to be a 35-year-old woman with no husband (or even no boyfriend, for that matter) who was still trying to figure out what she was supposed to do with her life. I'm pretty sure that my youthful mind pictured me with all of my mess together and enjoying life with the most loving and wonderful man there ever was.

Spoiler alert, kiddo: That didn't happen.

But what I've learned is that, even though life doesn't always happen the way I want it to, I can still enjoy it just as much. I don't need someone to be my everything—and neither do you. Yes, I would absolutely love for the man I love to love me back and for us to spend the rest of our lives together, but it's not a requirement to my happiness. It took a lot of years (and more than a lot of tears—and I'm not even a big crier) for me to realize that.

What's even more important, though, is that, along the way of learning that I'm fine on my own, I also learned that I am fine *as I am*. So many girls think they need to change the way they think, change the way they dress, change the music they listen to or TV shows they watch, change the jokes they think are funny, change their hair or makeup, change their interests, and change a number of other things so that they can catch the attention of certain guys, but that's all unnecessary work that we shouldn't be doing. I'll admit that I've fallen victim to that belief before, and it wasn't good. It's better to be the person you are and the person you want to be rather than someone you think someone else wants you to be.

And if that someone doesn't love you for who you truly are at the heart, then he isn't the one who should have your heart.

Let me tell you about one of those times when I thought I wasn't good enough just as I was. Let's take this one all the way back to my days in middle school, which I will forever argue is the absolute worst period of life—like, EVER.

I was a pretty good kid in school. I didn't get in trouble very often, except for talking too much (imagine that). Sure, I got detention almost every single day my sophomore year of high school because I had one teacher who gave out one-minute detentions each time you were talking when you weren't supposed to (mine added up far too quickly) or violated any of his other classroom rules, but I typically wasn't a frequent detention visitor.

In the sixth grade, however, I had multiple detentions, one of which never should have happened. I'm sure the others were justified—although, as a teacher, I don't ever remember giving out detentions for kids talking; I often encourage them to talk more. Regardless, my detentions were served, and I'm sure I learned zero valuable lessons from staring at a blank wall and thinking about all of the horrific drama in my life at the time that would obviously be the end of the world. That one detention, though, was one I will never forget—mainly because looking back at it now makes me realize what a complete fool I was.

I was in my math class, and I already had two strikes against me (three earned you a spot in after-school detention). There was a guy I had a crush on, and I knew he would be in detention that afternoon—let's just say you could guarantee that he'd be in there on any given day of any given week. I had already been warned once by my teacher that I needed to stop pretending my calculator was a phone to talk to my friend across the room (I was obviously extremely mature beyond my years), and if she had to say anything to me again, it would be a strike (although I think the punishment marks were probably called something else).

I had a moment to make a decision, and I went with what my rather foolish middle school unripened heart told me to do: I defied my teacher and called my friend on our fake calculator phones.

Do you know what happened next? I got detention and had to stay after school to serve it. You know who was there? The guy. You know what happened between us in detention?

Nothing. Nada. Zilch.

I was far too much of a pansy to say anything to him at all, so I just sat there and hoped that he realized that I was cool enough to be in detention just like him. I, too, could be a troublemaker. I remember feeling my face turn a deep tomato-shade of red when I thought I felt him looking at me. Was I sitting at a good angle? Did I look stupid sitting there? Should I cough or something? (I can't explain my thinking.) I got really nervous and decided I needed water. All of this stress was making me thirsty. I got up to go ask the teacher who got stuck with detention duty if I could go get a drink from the water fountain, and she denied me. Apparently kids in detention can't just leave the room so easily. I felt like I was doing my own short walk of shame back to my desk because I knew the bad-boy cutie had heard that conversation. It was a really small room. I had just made a novice move, and I probably looked like an idiot to him.

It bothers me now how I cared so much. I wasn't acting like me at all. I shouldn't have to think so much about what I should say or do or what things I did wrong or right for a guy to like me. I'm sure that it would have been tough to convince middle school Natalie of that, and I can't go back and change the past, but there really was no point in me worrying so much about someone else's opinion of me.

Let's skip right to the ending of this story: My feelings for him never amounted to anything—I never told him how I felt, and he never cared. It's for the best because that fella was definitely all wrong for me, but you couldn't convince me of that during that stage of my life. I was too busy trying to be someone I didn't even want to be but thought I had to be.

I wish I could tell you that's the only time I ever did something like that, but it would be a stone-cold lie. There was also a guy I got really close with in college (to the point where we hung out basically every single day), and I started listening to the music I knew he liked. Sure, it's fine to develop common interests and begin to like some of the same things as the people in your life, but when you feel like you have to force it on yourself, it's probably time to re-examine what you're doing.

I'm comfortable being me now—liking the things I like and not being ashamed of any of them—but it's taken some pretty tough moments of heart pain and later recognizing how silly I was acting to get to this point. I guess that's kind of what you're supposed to do in life, though: figure it all out as you go. While it would be nice to have a playbook with all of the answers for every single situation you ever face, you're often like a quarterback going shotgun and looking down the field with no plan whatsoever other than to avoid getting sacked.

And there's nothing wrong with that—because sometimes you simply have to launch that Hail Mary pass and be confident that the ball will end up where it's supposed to go.

3

When You Realize That Hiding Is Not the Answer

As I've mentioned, for much of my life—especially when I was a teenager—I was pretty terrified of letting guys know how I felt about them. And one time, I became so overcome with fear that I did something completely ridiculous (which was apparently a theme of my adolescence).

I was a freshman in high school at the time, and I had a pretty huge crush on a guy I'd known for a while—you will remember him from the previous chapter as the detention boy. Yes, I still had a crush on him from afar that I kept to myself. We grew up going to our brothers' baseball games together, but I NEVER wanted him to know how I felt. Like ever. I had obviously had a crush on him for years at this point (I'll never be able to explain it—he wasn't a good match for me), and I had been extremely successful at keeping my feelings hidden.

Looking back on it now, I should have just let him know. Yes, it's super scary and a huge deal (because everything is when you're that age) to do something like that in high school, knowing what the risks are and that you'll have to face him and the rest of your classmates he tells for four years of your life. But what I've learned is that it's so much better to live outside of that "I guess I'll never know" arena.

I'm not sure I ever had a shot with that adorable troublemaker, but I honestly won't ever know.

On that day during freshman year, I was on my way back from the restroom and walking to one of my classes, and the halls were completely empty. Zero people were in sight. Suddenly, I spotted one person at the end of the hall walking the opposite way as I was—and I instantly knew it was my rule-breaking cutie.

Oy vey! What should I do? Do I say hi to him or completely ignore him? Maybe I should just look his way and smile or give a head nod or something? Oh, geez, I don't know if I can handle this. If I look at him at all, HE WILL KNOW.

Don't ever call me a drama queen.

You know what I did? Rather than show any smidgen of gusto, I dodged into the nearest classroom, which happened to be a science class full of seniors. I stood with my back against the door as the entire room full of students and the teacher just stared at me, waiting for an explanation of some sort. All I could muster was an emphatic "just give me a minute." I waited until I knew my detention allure had gotten far enough away, I apologized to the teacher for interrupting her lesson, and then I hurried out to get back to my own class.

I wish I could tell you that there was some happy ending about how I eventually was able to speak to this fella, and we were one of those great high school couples. But if you've read this far, you know that I've never actually had a boyfriend, so that can't be true. Instead, I continued to be a coward. While it's probably for the best that I never dated him, I still wish I had been bold enough at least to talk to him every once in a while.

That's pretty much how my entire high school life went, though—I dodged as many encounters as I could that might reveal any form of giddiness to the guys I had crushes on back then. I realize now how completely silly I was being, but at the time, it seemed like my only logical option. After all, my mindset was that no guy could or would ever be interested in me the way I was in him. I mean, why would he be? I wasn't exceptionally beautiful and didn't even think I was remotely pretty, so I wasn't turning anyone's head, and I wasn't the girl any guy was chasing after.

Then something happened during my junior year that only made those feelings of inadequacy grow deeper than I ever should have allowed them.

I had a crush on a different guy, but, now that I think about it, he had a similar personality to detention boy. For some reason that I will never be able to explain, I decided to allow one of my friends to tell her boyfriend and then have him mention it to the guy who struck my fancy. My friends thought that it sounded like a solid plan, but I thought it was going to cause a massive earthquake to my somewhat content life.

In most situations, I prefer to be right—this was not one of them.

The day after my friend's boyfriend told him, I was in the class I had with my crush, and he and his best bud were standing over in a corner chatting and looking over at me. I felt my face become the same temperature as the sun probably, and I did my best to pretend that I was working on my assignment. Let's be real, though. I wasn't focusing on anything but what in the world they were saying and what he was going to do now that he knew the secret that I never really wanted him to know.

The guy he was chatting with and I had a mutual friend, and he told her something that she regrettably had to relay back to me: The guy I liked—the one who was supposed to be this really nice, funny guy who would be a great match for me—wanted to make fun of me. Let me repeat that in all caps. HE WANTED TO MAKE FUN OF ME FOR LIKING HIM.

Ladies, if any guy ever wants to ridicule you because of your feelings for him, walk away, and don't let it get under your skin. He doesn't belong in your life.

For me, with that weak self-confidence I had in this particular area of my life, it shattered me. Not only did I feel ugly and like an idiot, but now I truly felt like I wasn't worthy enough for anyone.

If this guy thought it was laughable for someone like me to have feelings for him, then who would think that I was good enough? *What was wrong with me?*

My friend, I cannot stress this enough: When that question pops into your head because some guy doesn't like you back, immediately push it away. There is *nothing* wrong with you. If you don't believe that, then please give me a call, and I will remind you that you are beautiful and loved.

I spent every single day for the rest of the trimester in that class with him feeling small. I wanted to hide like I had back in ninth grade when I dodged into that science classroom. I wanted to disappear from his view so that he wouldn't even have the chance to think about mocking me and mocking my heart's feelings that I wanted to take back from him.

It's easy for me to look back now and wish that I could have had the strength not to care as much—not to let his immaturity change the way I thought about myself. But I was a young girl in high school who had just had her heart crushed, and that was simply part of the process of me growing to be the woman I am now. I've had to endure some pain and heartache to be as confident and assured as I currently am. I know that I'm enough in the eyes of my Father, and that is more than enough for me.

Sure, I'm definitely still going to have those days when I feel uglier than the scariest trolls or even Beowulf himself, but I make conscious efforts to replace those negative thoughts with positive affirmations about myself.

Hey, Nat, your hair looks really great today.

You may not look as put together as the beauty beside you in the picture, but don't waste your time with comparisons. At least you kept your eyes open for this one—and look how blue they look!

I know that's not the outfit you wanted to wear, but you sure are wearing it!

Look at that smile of yours! It's so genuine and will light up any room you enter!

I think it's perfectly fine and even healthy to give yourself little pep talks every once in a while. And if that once in a while ends up needing to be every day, go for it, sister! Giving yourself compliments (in a healthy way, of course) doesn't make you conceited or narcissistic—it makes you believe that the person looking back at you in the mirror is beautiful and that *she is enough.*

You weren't made to hide and be afraid and live in constant anxiety. You were made to muster up every ounce of courage you can and live a bold life that challenges you to take risks and dare to love in big and powerful ways. Be *you*, and be confident in *who you are* and *Whose you are.*

Don't be the girl who darts into science classrooms. She lives in fear. Be the girl who walks proudly past anyone she encounters and is brave enough to flash her gorgeous smile and say "hey, how's it going?"

4

Because It's OK If You're Still a Virgin

I was 27 when I had my first (and only, really) kiss. I had always wanted it to happen in a very dramatic fashion in a gazebo or in the pouring rain in a parking lot, both of us upset but then realize that the reason we're really upset is because we're both so in love with each other, so we break the tension by making out in the rain.

It would have been perfect—and that's coming from someone who is shallow about her hair and typically doesn't like to mess with the rain.

It didn't exactly happen like that, though. Like, at all. For starters, I had a giant cheer bow in my hair (I was never a cheerleader) and was wearing a bright pink shirt and running shorts on a toasty August evening in Texas with zero percent chance of rain in the forecast. And we were at a local community track that was nowhere near a gazebo of any sort.

You know what, though? It was still special to me. Even though things obviously didn't end up working out with the guy I locked lips with for the very first time, it's one of those cute stories that I'll tell my nieces one day. I ended up getting hurt by him, but I think what hurt the most was the realization that the guy who had my first kiss wouldn't be the guy who had my last. (Or maybe he will if I stay this single for the rest of my life.) Maybe I was living in a fantasy world back then, but I really hoped that, because I had waited so ridiculously long to be kissed, my first kiss would be with my future husband.

It's for the best that he didn't up being that man, though. It looked like things were going somewhere for a little while, and then they suddenly weren't. That resulted in a heartache that was pretty painful for a couple of months, but everything changed in a literal instant. I remember sitting by the pool one scorching summer afternoon while I was reading a book by Robin Jones Gunn (you'll learn later just how much this woman I've never actually met has impacted my life in rather enormous ways), and it hit me: *Grace will give me freedom.*

I had been so hurt by him—and he probably didn't even realize it—that it made me a bit bitter toward him, and I didn't even want to hear his name said by any of our mutual friends. I had gotten over him but still hadn't gotten over all of the pain that he'd made me feel. So, in that moment of solitude at my apartment complex's pool, I prayed for God to let me forgive the smoocher, and I felt a physical and emotional change take place in my heart within a mere second. It was as if an actual weight of hurt and unforgiveness had been taken off of me, and I was free. I'm not a bitter person, and I don't hold grudges against people, and that period of my life was no time to start. That man was not my lobster (I hope you watched *Friends*, but if you didn't, please consult the Google regarding that term), and that was a good thing.

I used to think it was a little strange that it took so long for me to be kissed and that there was something about me that repelled the fellas. I felt pathetic knowing that I was the sole member of the Never Been Kissed (NBK), Never Been on a Date (Nuh-BO-AD), and Never Had a Boyfriend (Nuh-HAB) clubs that I essentially founded. I mean, even some of my most immature high school students I've taught have been more experienced than I am in that area of life. But now I realize that this is simply part of my story—part of what makes me *me*. And I'm sure that you've figured out by now that there's something else that's true about me.

Yes, I'm 35 years old, and I'm a virgin.

I know that sounds like an old age to be that inexperienced, but it's true, and I'm not ashamed to admit that. I'm close enough to living a real-life version of *27 Dresses*, so I might as well let the title *40-Year-Old Virgin* almost describe me, too. The older I get, the more thankful I am that some of the relationships I wished had happened didn't actually happen because I'm pretty sure they would have ended quickly, anyway, when the guys I had feelings for realized that I wasn't going to have sex with them.

It's kind of weird being a virgin today, especially as an adult. My purity is something I value and protect, and if I ever actually lasso in a husband, I hope that he will appreciate it.

In February of 2015, on a morning that will forever be ingrained in my memory, I had a gun pulled on me while I was out for my run. In the months of fear that followed, I wasn't frightened by the fact that someone could have killed me (he easily could have shot me but didn't) but by the idea that what I think he really wanted to do was rape me.

And, to me, that was scarier than dying.

For years now, I've struggled with kidney stone issues and had to have three surgeries for them in 2017. When I experienced my first kidney stone trauma (it was actually a month before the gun situation), before the doctor and nurses took a CT scan to know what it was, they thought that my pain had something to do with a possible pregnancy. I kept telling them that there was zero chance that I was pregnant and finally had to say (or probably yell) something along the lines of "unless another Messiah is coming, and I'm the new Mary, there's no chance that I'm pregnant!"

They all exchanged some uncomfortable looks and stopped doing painful tests that they finally realized were completely unnecessary.

A little later, one of the nurses was giving me some pain meds in the IV, and she had some follow-up questions to my previous little outburst.

Nurse: So, you're really a virgin?
Me (in too much pain to care about much of anything, including being polite, apparently): Yes, I'm not a liar.
Nurse: It's just hard to believe—that's all.
Me: Why?
Nurse: We don't see many women your age in here who are—or at least not ones who scream it out loud at male doctors.

So I guess I did yell it.

I know that not every girl or woman is going to make the same decision I've made, and I don't judge anyone for living differently than I do, but I'm going to stick to the promise I made myself so many years ago to wait until I marry the man I was always meant to be with to have sex. And, if I never fall in love and make those vows, then I guess I'll die a virgin, as well.

When I lived in California, there was one night when I went out with some friends, and we were at a swanky bar of some sort. Not too long after we had been standing outside on the large outdoor patio, some guy I had never seen before in my life came up from behind and hugged me. First of all, NO. Don't touch me. Then he asked me if I'm a real redhead and told me that there's only one way to find out.

That was his cue to leave.

It took a few minutes to get him away from us, but he finally left. If he had stayed any longer, I was probably going to punch him in the face. I'm sure that there are still some good guys out there, but it's moments like those that I'm thankful that I still have something that a guy like him hasn't taken from me.

I know that we all have different beliefs, and as I said before, I'm not judging anyone for anything, nor do I think that I'm better than anyone for the choices I've made. But I do want people to know that it's OK to wait. It's OK to live your life differently than others. It's OK to follow your own path, even if it seems to take you a lot longer to get somewhere.

I'm not sure if it's my fate in life to be single forever, but I really do hope to fall in love with a man who loves me back and shows me that love as often as he can. I hope to create memories together and support each other's dreams. I hope to hold hands and dance and laugh until our abs hurt. I hope to know in my heart that he's the man I've been hoping for and is the reason why I had to go through broken hearts and crushed hopes—because he's the one the Lord has been leading me to all along.

And he will be absolutely worth the wait.

5

When You're Comfortable Being Real

When I was 32 years old, I packed up my life in Dallas and moved to California. I'll go into much more detail about this later, but if you're wondering why the next two stories take place in good ol' SoCal, it's because I lived in Orange County for a little more than a year and a half of my life that I would not trade for anything. (Also, just to clarify, I was a teacher for seven years, then I worked in marketing for four years, and then I returned to teaching when I moved back to Texas.)

My brother was in San Diego one week for a work conference, so I drove down there on a Monday night to have dinner with him. It was very rare that any of my family members were in California, so I didn't mind making the trek on a work night.

When I got to his hotel (which was where the conference was, as well), he was at a networking event. I got tired of waiting in the lobby, so I decided to find out where he was exactly. I befriended some women who were at the check-in table, and one of them led me out to the terrace where the event was. After making my way about halfway around the area, I spotted him chatting with a few people and didn't want to interrupt. I had two options: I could stand around by myself and pretend to be looking at something interesting on my phone, or I could go talk to some of these people who probably didn't want to talk about the things I wanted to discuss with them (you know, like the non-work-related stuff).

I obviously chose the latter.

I joined in a conversation with Nader and Randy, two older gentlemen who were very interested in their roles in the healthcare industry. After I asked a bunch of questions about their personal lives, they asked me what I do for a living. I had a brief moment when I thought about fibbing a little and playing the part of someone in their line of work who belonged at the conference, but then I remembered that I don't like lying and that I've learned that it's always better to be yourself in every situation.

I told them that I was a proposal writer and was going to leave it at that, but they wanted to know more. I said I wrote for an infrastructure company, and they assumed it was hospital-related. I clarified and let them know that it was construction and infrastructure. Their facial expressions said exactly what I knew both of them wanted to say to me in that moment: *What on earth are you doing here?* So I smiled and then made Randy, who had transitioned his life to the Midwest, tell me all about his years of living in Texas.

I had quite a bit of fun chatting with them, even though they were probably skeptical from the start because I didn't have the same lanyards they did. They never actually asked why I was there, but I didn't pretend that I was part of their community. My brother eventually came over and told them I'm his sister, so I guess it really is a good thing that I didn't try to be someone I wasn't, because homeboy would have blown my cover for sure.

To reiterate, I hated middle school, and looking back on those years makes me dislike almost everything about the person I was back then. I was selfish and constantly trying to be someone I wasn't. I think that I was so insecure about who I really was that I was completely afraid to be me. I've accepted who I am now, and while it's healthy to grow and make changes in your life that are needed in order to better your life and your character, I think that it's also important to be comfortable being completely *you*—no matter how messy and imperfect that person is. We shouldn't hold back from being different from those around us—our differences are what make us unique.

You don't have to be afraid to be you. If you're always acting like someone you're not, then people will never really know the real you. For me, I want to know people fully and be fully known myself. I know that being open can place you in a rather vulnerable position, and there are certainly times to be a bit more guarded, but I think there's value in letting people know the real you—the one we don't necessarily see on Instagram. The one who doesn't have it all together. The one who admits to being flawed. The one who isn't afraid to say "this is who I am." It can also help others become more comfortable being more open with you, as well.

It doesn't mean that everyone will expect you to be completely real with them, and they might not know how to respond at times. Take the woman in the bathroom at my work later that same week as the San Diego networking event. She worked in the company next to mine, and I had seen her in there before, but she wasn't one of the ones I had gotten to know very well (I often had lunch with some of them and texted a few of them pretty regularly—bathrooms can really bring people together). Two of my buddies who worked with me had just jokingly insulted me, and I was not acting dramatic about it at all. When I walked into the bathroom, the exchange below occurred.

Me: *Hi! How's it going?*
Bathroom buddy: *I'm good. How are you?*
Me: *Hurt and betrayed (again, not said in an overly dramatic voice by any means).*
BB: *(stared at me confused for a few seconds and then turned and walked out).*

Neither of us was expecting what had just happened. I had to shrug it off. I'm not for everyone—and that's OK. You probably won't be for everyone, either. But if you pretend to be someone else, that person also won't be for everyone, so you might as well just stick with the original you.

~ ~

And it's also good to remember not to let those differences place you in the constant comparison trap.

Apparently I fall into that one when escape rooms and dog surfing competitions are involved

I went to my first escape room when I lived in Orange County, and I would like to commend the creator of these things because they're definitely a unique way to have fun with a group of people. I was running kind of late and was slightly frazzled when I arrived, so I didn't hear all of the instructions. When my friends and I were locked in the room, I sort of felt like I didn't know exactly what was going on, but everyone else seemed to be completely attuned with what to do.

People started finding clues right and left, while I sort of stumbled upon one or two by accident. At one point, I was just kind of walking around the room and feeling almost useless. I used to read a lot of Nancy Drew books, and I watch *Brooklyn Nine-Nine* on the reg, so I was a little disappointed to realize that the only really somewhat intelligent thing that I did was discover that one of the clues meant that we needed to look through the peephole of the door.

One thing that I did notice, though, was just how different each person's skillsets were. Our brains are all wired differently, which isn't a bad thing by any means. And that definitely proved to be a huge benefit for our group in the escape room because people's different perspectives and thought patterns all collaborated well together.

We ended up making it out of the room with a little more than nine minutes to spare, and I quickly got over the fact that I didn't feel like I did much, because I looked around at the people surrounding me and couldn't help but smile—they were my people, and they loved me whether I'm more of a Sherlock or a Watson (though I still think that I could be much more like a Sherlock).

And not having certain skills doesn't make you any less of a person.

Surfing dogs further reminded me of that two years in a row. I'm not joking when I say that the dog surfing competitions I watched in Huntington Beach essentially changed my outlook on life (if you live there or visit there in late September, YOU MUST GO). Each year, this epic event didn't disappoint. I watched the talented pups ride the waves in either with their owners or other dogs on their boards. It's one of the most entertaining spectacles you'll ever see.

One thing that I absolutely love about this competition is how much the dogs simply don't care about what the people think of their performances—whether they stay on their boards all of the way to the shore or crash and burn, they gleefully trot back on the sand and wag their tails, excited to go back out in the water for more runs.

Because they know that one setback or one flaw doesn't mean that they're not good enough.

We all have our gifts and passions, and they're not going to be the same as everyone else's. And they shouldn't be. There are many skills that I lack that I enjoy seeing other people have in abundance. I like knowing that my friend Ashley can help me with all things social media and can take absolutely anything and make it look adorable. I love that one time my friend JP was able to sew up a shirt I put a hole in for me so that I didn't have to staple it like I did the dress I ripped. I appreciate that my friend Dane could probably build seven computers in the amount of time that it takes some people to figure out how to turn them on. I'm thankful that my sister knows how to bake pies and make various other side items so that there are always enough dishes at Thanksgiving, and I can just show up empty-handed or with something store-bought.

Just because you can't do something as well as someone else doesn't mean that you aren't capable of some pretty wonderful things yourself. (After all, it's for the best that we're not all lining up to be on *The Voice*.) Your skills matter, and they can be used in incredible ways if you're not constantly focusing on the ones you don't have, instead. So don't forget to remind yourself every once in a while that you are talented, and you do bring value to others.

Because you're capable of much more than you know when you actually believe that's true.

You were made to be you and with the skills and talents you have on purpose. You're where you are right now for a reason. The experiences you've had—both good and bad, wonderful and trying—haven't been for nothing. Don't hide behind a pretty life filter. Don't pretend to be someone you're not, even if that means that you're quite different from everyone around you.

Because different can be truly beautiful.

6

Because You Can Unapologetically and Unashamedly Be You

It's interesting to me that it can be so tough for us to apologize when we know we're wrong, but other "I'm sorry" statements are so simple to make.

Like when we have no real reasons to be apologizing.

When you hurt someone or wrong someone in some way, there's a need to say you're sorry. Perhaps you have to cancel plans on someone or are running late somewhere and send an apology text—there's nothing wrong with that. But there are other times when you might say you're sorry for something for which you really shouldn't have to apologize.

Especially if what you're doing is simply *being you*.

I remember reading an article a couple of years ago that mentioned how women often apologize for things in the business/office setting that they shouldn't be—things like speaking up in meetings or presenting ideas that would bring about potential changes and innovations. (I don't know if men do this as often, but the article focused mainly on women.) Ever since then, I've tried to be more aware of times when I might be saying sorry and not actually meaning it.

I eat Wheat Thins with everything and at every meal. I love

them with my whole being. I have them with me at all times—there's always a box in my car, and I carry a sandwich bag of them with me in my purse. Yes, I do casually bust them out at the dinner table in public places. I remember going to dinner with some new friends a little more than a year ago, and when I got my Wheat Thins out, I said "sorry, I eat them at every meal." As soon as that first word came out of my mouth, I immediately regretted it. I wasn't sorry. At all. So now I make sure that I never apologize for having Wheat Thins when I'm eating.

Because I'm not sorry for being me.

I don't believe that eating my favorite food hurts anyone, even if other people think it's bad manners. I didn't go to cotillion at any point in time, and I've never been that great with societal protocol and expectations, anyway.

Have you ever noticed yourself saying sorry for something for which you really had no reason to apologize? Have you ever said sorry for bothering someone when what you're about to say is really no bother at all? Have you ever apologized for not being perfect? I'm not sure why we do this. We have the abilities to speak our minds and share our hearts and go after our dreams, and we don't have to be sorry for any of that. You do you, boo.

And in the same way that we shouldn't be apologizing for being ourselves, we shouldn't expect other people to be sorry for the unique individuals they are—we should be giving them love and encouragement and room to continue to grow so that they can be comfortable being themselves, too.

I was speaking to the junior high students at my church in Orange County one Sunday morning and was focusing on the topic of accepting others and loving them not just in spite of their differences from us but also *because* of those differences. I thought back to when I was in middle school and how I was an absolutely horrible example of that. I didn't know Jesus yet, and I was very selfish and far too concerned with what people thought of me and what I thought of others. It's not a time of my life that I'm proud of by any means.

I've said this before, and I stand by it: Middle school is the worst period of life. It's such an easy time to be mean and judgmental, and you're still trying to figure out who you are and what life is and what's "cool" and what's not, and you have no idea as to what the genuine and important things in the world are yet. I'm sure that there are some mature kids in that stage of life who are rare gems, but for the most part, it's a painful and awkward stage that we all have to go through as a rite of passage into (hopefully) becoming more mature adults who are concerned with more than popularity and what brands of clothing you're allowed to wear and which ones are faux pas.

You know what, though? Even though that period of life can be rather superficial and unwelcoming, being an adult doesn't suddenly become easier just because you're no longer begging your parents for Doc Martens and wearing overalls with only one side buttoned because it looks so much cooler (you feel me, 90s middle schoolers??). Even when you get older, it can still be tough to feel like you're accepted and like you belong, and there will still be people who judge you and make you want to apologize without even knowing why you're claiming to be sorry. But if you're not doing anything wrong, you have no reason for those apologetic words.

Because you don't have to be sorry for being you.

I'm going to keep checking myself to make sure I'm not starting sentences off with "I'm sorry, but" and then following that statement with something for which I feel no actual sorrow. I won't ever be sorry for eating Wheat Thins with froyo (best meal ever). I won't ever be sorry for having an idea and wanting to share it. I won't ever be sorry for wanting a turn to speak at a meeting. I won't ever be sorry for telling a guy that I have feelings for him. I won't ever be sorry for having the passions and dreams I have. And I won't ever be sorry for not being other people's opinions of me.

When you need to make improvements or changes in your life

or your behavior or your attitude or whatever, make them. If you've hurt people or have legitimate reasons to say you're sorry, make those apologies. At the end of the day, though, I hope that you're confident in the person you are and the person you strive to be, and I hope that you never apologize for the things that need no sorries to go along with them.

Because you don't have to be sorry for being you.

I have some friends who don't agree with me that you can wear anything with confidence and essentially make it match. That's fine—they don't have to think I'm right. That won't stop me from believing it and living that way, though.

After all, who makes the matching standards in this world?

Who decided one day that pink can't be combined with red? Who said a black belt doesn't go with brown shoes? And who really cares who said those things? They're all opinions, anyway, so if you think something matches with something else, then it matches. The end.

The ever poetic and insanely talented former Dallas Cowboy Deion Sanders once said that "if you look good, you feel good. If you feel good, you play good. If you play good, they pay good." I like to overlook the lack of adverbs and then focus on the first two sentences (because I'm not really talking about making money right here, but perhaps that part pertains to you, so go with it, and do your thing).

If you're confident in the way you look, you're likely going to feel a lot better about yourself in general. I know that having on an uncomfortable outfit or something I wish I had left in my closet—or maybe even on the rack at Target—doesn't make me feel like I'm about to conquer the world. And, the better you feel, the more likely you are to perform well at whatever it is that you're doing. Maybe that's work. Maybe that's being a mom. Maybe that's cooking for your husband or boyfriend or for yourself. Maybe that's sitting on your couch watching television. Maybe that's going to a friend's wedding. Maybe it's just plain living your life. It doesn't mean you're dressed to the nines or fancy or looking like you just stepped out of the salon instead of just rolled out of bed—it simply means that you feel good because you look good because that look was something that *you* decided, not something that you felt compelled to wear because of the expectations or standards that likely constantly surround you.

One December while I was living in Orange County, I was asked to pray at the annual women's Christmas brunch at my church. I was really excited to attend because I had never been to the event before and was looking forward to meeting and connecting with more of the women I had probably seen often but didn't necessarily know personally.

The morning of the brunch, however, I was a complete wreck. I rarely cry, so when I do, I've been bottling up way too much for far too long, and it's like Niagara Falls has decided to ungracefully cascade down my soon-to-be red splotchy face. In short, it's the ugliest of ugly crying. My eyes turn a much prettier shade of deep blue (it's always good to try to find at least one positive in a sea of negative), but the rest of me looks pretty not pretty.

That particular morning, I don't know what exactly triggered it, but it suddenly hit me that I was pretty sure that I was being called to move back to Texas. I was already running slightly late to meet with my sweet friend Deenna before going to the brunch, and I arrived at Starbucks hoping that I could compose myself. I failed. I couldn't do it. My precious friend let me cry and talked everything through with me, and even though I started to feel better, I couldn't stop crying. It's as if there was a stirring in me that knew a big life change was right around the corner, and there was part of me that wanted to resist it. Sure, I missed my family and was pretty certain that I eventually wanted to move back to Texas, but I had just started to become comfortable in California.

And sometimes being comfortable means that it's time for a drastic change to occur.

Deenna prayed with me and promised to continue to walk alongside me as I prayed about what God was doing in my heart and in my life. I left that Starbucks with puffy red eyes and the inevitable splotchy look covering my face. The last thing I wanted to do was be around a bunch of people, but at the same time, I thought that it might actually be a bit healing to my soul.

As soon as I walked into the fancy country club where the brunch was held, I realized that I was very underdressed compared to everyone else. I looked around and saw women in beautiful holiday dresses with cute festive earrings and lovely hair. I walked in with my jeans with holes in them, a blue sweatshirt that was more than a little wrinkled, and hair that hadn't been washed in a week. At least I was wearing my Toms with the Christmas lights on them.

I had a choice to make: I could be embarrassed by what I was wearing, or I could simply embrace it. When I had gotten ready for the day that morning, I had intentionally put on an outfit that was comfortable—an outfit that was me. So as I looked around the room, I decided that I looked good, and I was going to let that help me to feel good. I was confident in my hole-y jeans and non-holiday-colored sweatshirt, and it was perfectly fine that my hair was in a half-up topknot, because that's just who I am sometimes.

I didn't match the rest of the room, but I matched who I am.

You're not always going to look like everyone else, and that's perfectly fine. What you like or what makes you comfortable won't always match the opinions of others, and that's also perfectly fine. If someone tells you that something you're about to wear clashes with something that you're already wearing, but you disagree, go ahead and wear what you want with pride, sister.

YOU DO YOU, BOO.

And remember that anything matches if you wear it with confidence.

SECTION 2

NO MATTER WHAT ANYONE MAKES YOU THINK, YOU ARE ALREADY DEEPLY LOVED

When You're Not Meant to Love
the Guys You Think You Should

Have you ever been the last kid picked to play sports on the playground? Honestly, I never have. I played most sports and am generally rather athletic, so I was usually one of the first ones picked. I always felt sympathy for the kids who didn't get picked anywhere close to first—you could usually see a bit of hurt on their faces, even if they did try to laugh it off or act like it wasn't a big deal.

I never had that feeling on the playground, but I've had that feeling so many other times in my life—being the last girl any guy would ever pick. It's a truly lonely feeling, and it makes me ask myself or the air around me far too often *"What is wrong with me?"*

Sweet friends, I will say this to you again: If you've ever asked yourselves that same question, please let me remind you that *there is nothing wrong with you.* Just because you've watched your friends find boyfriends and husbands doesn't mean that they have some special quality that you don't. It simply means that they're taking the paths they're supposed to take in life, and you're taking your own, as well. All of our timelines aren't the same, and that's not a bad thing by any means. It's actually for our own best interests.

But that doesn't mean it's easy. In fact, it's the polar opposite of that a lot of the time. I can't tell you how many occasions I've told my sister that I just want someone to pick me out of every other girl in the world. I want someone to love me for the quirky person I am and make sure that I can feel how much he cares for me. There's an old-school Ty Herndon country song called "She Wants to Be Wanted Again" that I feel I can relate to much of the time. If you don't know the song, consult the Google. Yeah, that's me over here (insert hand-raising girl emoji), minus the "again" part since it hasn't actually happened before.

I'd say I'm pretty confident in most areas of my life, and I honestly don't care what people think of me in terms of what I wear or how ridiculous I look when I dance or things of such nature. But when it comes to guys, for so long it was as if all of that confidence was sucked away, and I became this insecure I-don't-know-what-to-say-or-do-with-my-hands creature. I was so caught up in what each fella I had feelings for thought that I wasn't able to be who I actually am all of the time. I was too reserved and worried about appearing dumb or ugly or whatever might be considering unappealing, and I let those insecurities take over my mind.

I don't like the power guys can have on our thoughts—and most of the time they probably don't even know that they have that power. Or maybe they do. I don't actually know. But I do know that I wish that I could look every single girl in the world in the eyes and tell her that she doesn't need acceptance from someone else to be sufficient. It doesn't come from someone else. It comes from Jesus. I wish that I could tell every girl that she's already been picked by the One who matters most. And I wish that I could hug every single girl and assure her that she is loved just as she is, and she doesn't need to change anything about her in order to be more beautiful or worthy of someone's love.

My dear friend, you're already beautiful, and you're already worthy.

I'm well aware that this is sometimes something of which I need to remind myself, as well. It's tough to feel like you're taking on the world all alone simply because you don't have someone holding your hand and kissing you in gazebos. It's frustrating to sit at home all alone on Saturday nights or dance by yourself at weddings or be the only single person at a couples dinner party (which has happened to me on more than one occasion). But those situations certainly aren't the end of everything, and they don't mean that you are any less of a person than anyone else. They're often character-building moments (at least that's what I like to tell myself), and you can absolutely enjoy them whether you're single or not.

What have always been disheartening for me, though, are the times when I thought I was meant to be with guys who weren't actually the right ones for me. It hurts when you invest time and emotions into people, even if you aren't actually dating, and develop feelings, only to be left with your heart hurting and wondering why on earth you are having to go through the pain that follows the end of something that never actually was and never actually will be.

For me, it feels like it's been a series of heart hopes and feelings that were so wonderful before those hopes came crashing down like a pretty chandelier about to shatter all over the place in more pieces than you think you're capable of picking up. There was the boy in detention. There was the boy who wanted to make fun of me. There was the guy who told my friends that he was going to ask me to prom and led me to believe that he liked me like I liked him and then went with one of my friends, instead. There was a guy I spent a lot of time with during my senior year of high school whom I thought I might actually fall in love with one day.

And then it feels like the pain only magnifies as you get older and become more aware of your feelings and are able to feel them even more deeply than you were when you were a teenager in high school.

There was the guy at church in college who had recognized me from the same campus bus we used to ride. He who used to flirt with me and one night even told me how pretty he thought my eyes are. He called me to ask me to hang out one night on a night that I had already told him was super important because of a huge college football matchup that I need to watch on television. I told him that I already had plans to watch the game but that a different day would work. He stopped coming to talk to me on Sundays, and I never heard from him again. I'm pretty sure that he stopped riding our bus, too. (Yes, I do understand now that I probably should have invited him to watch the game with me, but I was—and still am—rather inexperienced and didn't think of that. And he didn't pursue me after, which only led me to believe the lie that I wasn't worth any effort.)

There was my best guy friend in college with whom I spent more time than anyone and, naturally, I started to develop feelings for him pretty quickly. There were so many things about him that I thought were perfect for me, but I was also blinded by the strong feelings that I couldn't control to realize that we weren't right for each other for one reason that should have been a rather alarming red flag for me: I didn't feel like I could completely be myself around him. I'm a pretty goofy and quirky gal, and I wasn't confident enough to let that side shine through most of the time. Our friendship fizzled out when someone told him how I felt about him. He brought it up to me, and I distanced myself because I was scared. I don't think that he ever felt the same way, but we might have kept our friendship going if I had at least been willing to address my feelings and actually hear what he had to say. But, instead, I ran.

There was the guy who told me that he had to take care of some chores when I asked him to go to a football game with me. On a Friday night. He was 27. I would have much rather him just told me that he wasn't interested. Chores? That's basically the equivalent of "I have to wash my hair." Oy vey.

There was the kisser, whom I mentioned previously. Again, it's for the best that we went separate directions in life, and from what I understand, he has a family now and is doing very well in life, and I'm genuinely happy for him.

And then there was my most recent broken heart that was an actual broken heart. It's almost as if the hurts I had before were all just little chips compared to it. It's hurt for a long time, and I keep praying that it will stop. One day it will. For now, though, I let it serve as a reminder that even the toughest times need to be filled with trust and patience and knowing that God is still with me in the storms. He's still with me in the darkness. He's still with me when it feels like the rest of the world has turned and walked away, and I feel alone and abandoned. He's still with me when I feel like no one in the world could ever possibly love me.

Because He's always with me—and He always loves me.

I don't tell you of all of the non-relationships I've ever had so that you can feel sorry for me or so that I can take some time to feel sorry for myself. I don't tell you because I'm upset with these guys, because I'm not. None of them is my lobster, and that's that. I tell you to remind you that you are already loved—*deeply loved*. No matter where you are in life or what you've done or what your relationship status is or isn't, you are deeply loved by the One who will never fail you, never forsake you, never leave you, and never let you down. And it's not true that you can never say never, because *He will **never** do any of these things.*

His love is a love so big and so grand that we can't explain it and can't even understand it. I mean, why would the God of the entire universe, the One who created every living and breathing creature on this entire planet, love someone like me? Someone who is flawed. Someone who is imperfect. Someone who continues to mess up day after day. Someone who struggles with stress and anxiety. Someone who has struggled with doubt. Someone who has let fear consume her. Why?

He just does—I can't explain it, and I certainly can't understand it. But I trust it.

Don't let other people make you think that you aren't loved. You already are. Yes, it hurts to have your heart broken and to know that someone out there for whom you care so deeply that it actually physically hurts doesn't love you back, but take comfort in the fact that God is legitimately with you in those times (that's not just a trite expression), and He's going to stay with you when you're crying out to Him or simply crying your eyes out. Your value and your identity aren't found in other people, because other people are going to let you down. We're humans, after all.

But I promise you that He will never let you down. He's always with you—and He always loves you.

8

Because People's Opinions of You Don't Determine Your Worth

I don't think that I had ever been rejected without actually being interested in someone first until one fateful afternoon in a Southern California Sprouts.

At the time, I was trying to process what had been a really rough afternoon. My work situation was not good, and I was hoping that the rest of the evening would not involve any instances that would make me feel just plain blah.

But it turned out that my wish for a Pollyanna ending to the day would have to wait.

I was getting some gummy bears out of the large candy bins, and some fella was in the same area. He made a comment along the lines of "that's a lot of candy for someone your size" (to quote Kelly Kapoor and Dr. Mindy Lahiri: "How dare you?"), and I told him that I'm just really passionate about gummies. But then I felt the need to promote the Sprouts gummy bears. People, if you haven't tried them, please do so soon. Then I also recommended that he try the penguin gummies at Trader Joe's because their tummies are filled with a gooey center. I made sure to remind him, though, that the golden bag of HARIBO bears always wins in the end.

Let me get one thing clear here that you might or might not

already know about me: I love talking to people. I tend to strike up conversations with strangers on the regular, no matter where I am and with whom I'm talking. I just really like people.

Apparently this one thought I liked him a bit too much.

"Thanks for letting me know. But before this conversation goes any further, you seem sweet and cute in your own little way, but I just want to say that I'm not really looking for anything right now."

Wait, what? Complete misunderstanding, bud.

I said the first thing that popped into my head that wasn't insulting: "Good to know. But I'm not really looking for anything right now but good gummy bears."

I've been rejected before, but at least I usually made efforts in those instances. All I had to do for this man to kick me to a curb I had no intentions of encountering was make mere conversation about one of the best candy options out there. Really, guy?

If this had happened years ago, I think I would have been more bothered by his immediate response to turn me down, especially with the whole "cute in your own little way" comment. That didn't really get to me, though—I was more disturbed by the fact that I couldn't even have a conversation with a guy without him thinking that I was hitting on him. I suppose I should appreciate his honesty, but perhaps he should have waited to make sure that I was actually interested in him before telling me that I'm not the one who can capture his heart.

(By the way, I will say that this fella was attractive, but I wasn't attracted to him. It makes sense.)

I know that my level of singleness hasn't changed since I was in the womb—and that can be a bit defeating at times, especially as everyone around me continues to get married and start families—but that is certainly no reason to get upset about yet another guy not wanting to pursue me. I mean, I need someone who is actually going to care a little bit more about my love for gummy bears, anyway. He wasn't that guy.

And neither was the guy I never actually met but who basically decided I wasn't for him after he saw my picture.

One of my friends gave me his number because she thought he would be a good match for me. While I would have preferred for him to have my number, instead, he apparently knew that his friend was giving me his number and that I'd be reaching out.

I thought about not texting him, but then I remembered that dignity is overrated, and I honestly had nothing to lose by sending a text to some guy I had never met. What ensued was one of the most boring conversations known to man. When I reached out, he replied and then sent a selfie so that I could "put a face with a name." I thought that was a little interesting, but maybe it's normal or something, so I sent him a picture of me with my nieces (and clarified that they were my nieces). After that, there was not much said at all. I get that it was kind of a weird situation, but he did know about me from his friend, and he easily could have kept the conversation going. He chose not to, though.

I then had a choice to make: I could get upset at the realization that he had seen my picture and decided that he wasn't interested, or I could say "meh, oh well" and get on with my life.

Thankfully, I chose the latter. If this had been years ago, I probably would have gotten upset about that guy not thinking that I'm pretty and started to feel uglier than I already believed myself to be. Sadly, it's fairly easy to fall into that trap. But I've spent too much time trying to figure out why I've been single this long, and I don't want to do that anymore. I'd rather continue to trust that this everlong season (or lifetime—whatever) of singleness is with purpose and that I'll meet the man I'm supposed to love and be loved by forever when I'm supposed to meet him.

The past heartaches don't have to have a grip on me if I don't let them. What people think of you or don't think of you can't influence the way you think of yourself if you don't let it. The remarkably feisty Detective Rosa Diaz (if you're not a *Brooklyn Nine-Nine* fan, please rethink your life decisions) once told Detective Jake Peralta that he shouldn't let other people's opinions get in the way of what he wants. She makes a valid point—what other people think shouldn't dictate the way you live.

And that made me think about a certain guy who turned my world upside down with the mere flash of his smile.

For a while, he cared about the things I liked, and he cared about what I thought about him. He cared about me (or so I thought), and I cared about what he thought about me. I don't like caring what people think, though I know we often care about what the people we care about think of us (that was a mouthful). However, there's a difference between caring and letting those opinions change your own opinions of yourself or help to define who you are in any way.

I don't like saying this, but he made me feel like I wasn't enough sometimes—probably without even knowing he was doing it. *And I let him.* I let what he thought of me (or what I thought he thought of me) and his words and actions heavily influence the things I believed about myself. And when he suddenly didn't seem to care about me anymore, I immediately wondered what was wrong with me. I don't particularly like admitting that, because I don't particularly like that one person had so much influence on the way I saw myself. *I am enough* as I am, and no one's opinion of me or treatment of me can change that *at all*.

Ever.

I'll never forget the conversation I had with my cousin Rachel (whom I admire and respect in so many ways) at Thanksgiving that year. The broken heart was still very fresh, and I stood in front of her on the verge of tears in my aunt's and uncle's driveway and uttered four words that no woman should ever ask herself or anyone because of how some guy made her feel: *"What's wrong with me?"* And I'll never forget how, before wrapping her arms around me, Rachel made me look her in the eyes as she reminded me that nothing is wrong with me, and I should never let anyone else make me feel like there is.

I think of that moment often because I know that she's right.

It's not what someone else thinks of me that's important—it's what I think and believe about myself that truly matters. **If I don't believe I'm worthy of love, that's a much bigger issue than some guy thinking I'm not attractive enough to be his type.**

When I was living in California, my friend Hannah and I were on our way home from Laguna Beach one gorgeous Saturday afternoon, and we were singing Disney songs at the top of our lungs in her car. I'm not even close to being a good singer, but that didn't stop me from singing as if I'm actually Mariah Carey's soul sister. Hannah didn't care about that, though, and that's the way it should be. We should be comfortable being ourselves at all times—whether we're on excursions with our friends or in a room full of people we don't know yet. I don't have to win my friends' hearts, and I don't need to try to win any guy's heart, either.

He should want me to have it for free.

Don't let other people control your own view of yourself. You were made uniquely and purposely to be the person you are, and you don't have to be ashamed of or defend yourself for being who you're meant to be. I can tell you firsthand that it's incredibly freeing to be able to be comfortable with who you are rather than constantly trying to figure out what you need to change about yourself to be more acceptable. It's a waste of your time and energy, and you'll enjoy life so much more if you simply embrace who you are and invest that time and energy into pursuing your passions and loving others as they are.

The same way that you should be loved.

I hope that you never let someone else's words or actions toward you make you feel like you're not enough. No matter what anyone else thinks, you're worthy of love and capable of love. Please don't forget that.

And please don't let that determine how many gummy bears you get at Sprouts.

9

When You're Not the One Walking down the Aisle

Weddings have always been a little tough for me. I've been in 19 and have attended more than I can count. While I'm incredibly happy for the bride and groom at each one, there's still always a little part of me inside that wonders if I'll ever have a wedding of my own.

I remember a moment when, after I served as a bridesmaid for the 11th time, a coworker at the time joked with me by saying "always the bridesmaid, never the bride, huh?" While I know that person meant it in a joking way and not to be a stake to the heart, it still stung a little bit. Or a lot a bit.

Mainly because it's been consistently true.

I love being able to stand by my friends on what is usually, at the time, the most significant days of their lives. I love being able to help the brides with their trains on their dresses, hold their flowers for them during the ceremonies, give them genuine and meaningful toasts during the receptions, and help to ensure that everyone knows what the plans are for the sendoffs at the very end of the celebrations.

At every single wedding I've been to and been a part of, though, there's always a moment—one significant almost-drawing-the-tears moment—when I selfishly wonder if I will ever be the one to put on the white dress. If I'll ever be the one to walk down the aisle to a man whose face is beaming with the most authentically in-love smile you've ever seen anyone have. If I'll ever be the one to speak the vows I carefully wrote for the one man who will have my heart forevermore. If I'll ever be the one to know without a doubt in my mind that I just made the best decision of my life. If I'll ever be the one to have to think about going to the Social Security office and waiting in line to change my last name. If I'll ever be the one to commit my life to someone who genuinely desires to spend the rest of his days waking up to me right next to him.

And I let myself endure that moment at each wedding, praying that I get through it without crying and dwelling on it—without letting that one single moment keep me from being fully present and rob me of the joy that I should be focusing on for the people I love, instead.

A wedding is a wonderful celebration of two people committing to spend the rest of their lives together, but it's honestly not always necessarily the best place for a single girl to find herself, especially if she's already hurting. A broken heart is far too easily reminded of what it doesn't have. If you're single and wondering if you're ever going to find your lobster, please know that you don't have to be the one in the white dress to be complete. Remember: Your value and your identity aren't found in other people. You aren't defined by whether you're single or married or whatever—no matter what the IRS says on its paperwork.

I haven't always known that truth, but I'm completely confident in it now. Sure, there's a desire in my heart to love and be loved and get married and build a life with someone for the rest of our lives, but I don't know if that's what God has lined up for me. I'm going to keep praying for it and praying for joy in whatever God intends for me with the hope and belief that my lobster is out there, but I'm also not going to let myself think any less of who I am as a person if that all doesn't end up happening. I'm not going to let being single stop me from enjoying even those moments on my own that people are used to enjoying together.

But it's taken some painful seasons to get to this point.

A few years ago, there was a guy in my life who captured my heart in a way that no one else ever had and made my heart feel things that it had never felt. To make a really long story short and not descriptive at all, he broke my heart into a million miniscule pieces right before moving a thousand miles away. Not too long after that happened, I went to the wedding of one of my dear friends who had gone through somewhat of a roller coaster that finally ended in a wonderful love story with her forever fella. It was slightly depressing sitting there all alone (I only knew a handful of people there and didn't see them until later). Not long into the ceremony, I considered leaving right before the reception started. Then I remembered that I love to dance, and I should never let my solo status keep me from dancing. Ever.

That night, I let my heart embrace the dance floor. When Whitney Houston's "I Wanna Dance with Somebody" started playing during the reception, it hit me: This is why it had been so tough lately. I really do want somebody who loves me to dance with me. I want somebody who picks me out of everyone else in the world. I want somebody who cares when I'm hurt and tries to make me laugh when I'm upset. I want somebody who appreciates my quirks. I want somebody to want to love me and want to be loved by me. And, just like my soul sister Whitney wanted, I want somebody who'll take a chance on a love that burns hot enough to last.

I don't know if that will actually happen, but I don't think there's anything wrong with admitting that it's something I hope for in my life.

Maybe you've already found your person. Maybe you're still waiting or searching. Maybe you're not and are content. Regardless, I think it's important never to miss out on the opportunities you have right before you simply because you might have to do them on your own. Life really does go by far too quickly, and there are only so many chances to seize moments right in the midst of them and live a life of passion without caring what other people think of you.

So if you want to dance, for the love, get out there and dance.

That's what helped to get me through my sister's wedding just months before this, too—well, that and being surrounded by the people who always know how to make me happy. I adore my sister and was thrilled for her that she had found such a wonderful man and was about to commit to spending the rest of her life with him. But, at the same time, I was hurting inside. It was the second time in my life a guy had told me he'd be my wedding date and then backed out.

One of the worst parts about this one was that my sister had gotten excited for me and told all of her friends that I was bringing the guy I had feelings for as my date to her wedding. Those girls, who have been friends with my sister for what seems like forever, know that I've never had anything close to a relationship (or even a real date at that time), so they were eager to meet him and see me have a plus-one for once.

Instead, on the day of her wedding, I had to explain to them why I was actually flying solo on my sister's big day—and that hurt.

But it was her special moment to share with all of her people, and I wasn't going to let one broken heart get in the way. I put on my big-girl pants (or fancy bridesmaid dress), I stood by my sister, I gave a toast that came straight from my heart, I watched my sister smile more than she had in probably every smiling instance of her life combined, and I danced. I enjoyed an evening full of family and friends and people who were complete strangers to me, and I spun around with my mom and sister as we were the only ones on the dance floor during Wilson Phillips' classic "Hold On."

And it's a night that I'll cherish in my heart's memory forever.

I don't remember it because I was going through pain; rather, I remember it because it was a night that gave me hope that, not only does true love exist, but it comes in ways that aren't always in the form of boyfriends or husbands. It comes from the people in our lives who would stand by us through anything and cheer us on, whether we're winning the race or in dead last. It's the people who know everything about you and still love you. It's the people who define "ride or die."

It's the people who are *your people*.

I encourage you to find your people and to love them well—to hold on to them and always make sure that they know just how much you care about them. Love is bigger than all of us, and it doesn't exist solely in romantic relationships.

10

Because Holidays Can Be Tough

I love almost everything about Christmas—the scents that permeate throughout the air, the general feeling of love spreading everywhere, the beautiful lights bringing life to homes and streets, and the togetherness that becomes so integral.

But that togetherness aspect can also cause a lot of pain—especially when you feel like you don't have it all together as much as you hoped you would by now.

Quite honestly, the holidays are the best (and by "best," I obviously mean "worst") time for a single gal to feel lonely. You look around, and almost everyone you know is coupled off and enjoying holiday festivities together. The Hallmark Christmas movies all end perfectly for the women who suddenly fall in love and realize that they've found their lobsters. The TV commercials all feature families or people in love getting each other new cars and doing all of the things together. Target puts out an entire section called "MATCHING FAMILY PAJAMAS" and not "MATCHING SINGLE GIRL PAJAMAS" or simply "MATCHING PAJAMAS." (I love you with my entire heart, Target, but I cannot thank you for that sucker punch right now.)

It's crazy to me that you can be filled with complete joy and surrounded by people you love yet still feel so alone and even a little (or maybe a lot) sad at the exact same time. I love seeing my sweet nieces experience the magic of Christmas yet not fully understand what it truly is. And watching *The Grinch* or *Christmas Vacation* or any of the *Pitch Perfect* films or really any movie with my sister. And my parents having a stocking ready for me as my mom reminds me that Santa comes to their house every year and that he was confused that I don't live there anymore, so he left my stocking there so that my parents could give it to me. (I'm 35, Mare. I've known for years.) And simply *being* there with all of my people.

But even togetherness with family can remind me that I'm the only one there who showed up all by myself.

I know that I'm not alone in all of my feelings of being alone during the Christmas season. There are many people out there who either don't have families or aren't close with their families or aren't able to be with their families for the holidays in certain years or perhaps even every year. It's tough. But I have to remind myself of something that a friend once helped ingrain in my mind: I CAN DO HARD THINGS. You can, too—whether that means getting through the holidays alone or getting through the holidays with your people. We are in each holiday season and in the different seasons of our lives for reasons we might not know right now or maybe even ever. We just need to remember that we are where we need to be—and trust that we will get through even the toughest and darkest times.

When I first moved to California in 2017, I felt very alone. I knew zero people, and I basically begged anyone I met to be my friend. I invited almost every breathing human I met to go to coffee, and I hate coffee. You know what, though? After I moved out there—and after a few months filled with loneliness, tears, and questions to God of what on earth I was doing there—I experienced some of the most powerful love that I had ever felt in my entire life.

And it didn't come from a man.

Time and time again, God reminded me of who He is and who I am in Him. He reminded me that I am loved. He reminded me that I am valued. He reminded me that I matter. And He surrounded me with so many incredible people who poured into me and invited me (or let me invite myself) into their lives. I truly believe that that's one of the reasons He called me out there—to remind me of how absolutely loved I am by Him, the Creator of the entire universe. He knew exactly how and where this needed to happen. I questioned it at first, but as usual, He showed up big time and showed me once again that it's always best simply to trust Him from the get-go.

Years ago, I started sending out Christmas cards to my people. I LOVE Christmas cards and began getting more of them as my friends all started getting married and creating families. (Side note: This may sound mean, but pics of crying babies in Santa's lap are some of my personal faves, so always feel free to send those my way. I can see why they're crying—you put them in these men's laps who are complete strangers and have what babies might see as scary beards and then expect them to smile. No, thank you.) I decided that me not having a husband and dogs or kids wasn't going to stop me from making cards, too. It's become one of my favorite annual traditions, and I get excited about coming up with new ideas for what to put on my cards each year.

Because you can't let unfulfilled hopes stop you from living a life filled with joy.

And that's true even after the Christmas season ends, and Target starts putting out all of its Valentine's Day decorations—you know, for the one holiday that absolutely screams YOU ARE SINGLE!

I don't like Valentine's Day. I never have. It's not because I'm a bitter old hag who wishes that she had a man on that holiday. It's because there is such a big deal made about plans for that day and what gifts to give your significant other and all of these extravagant "romantic" gestures that might not really be that romantic.

We should be loving people every single day, not solely one day out of the year. And, if I ever do find that lobster of mine, I don't want him to feel pressured to buy me chocolate or jewelry or flowers (I don't like any of those things, anyway) to try to show me that he cares. Those things don't matter to me. I hope that he'll consistently show me that he cares in ways that mean more to me (my love language is quality time), and I don't want him to think that he needs to do anything different or more special because the calendar told him to do so.

While I have obvious negative feelings toward Cupid's favorite day of the year, it doesn't make facing it any easier each February. I love hearts—like borderline obsessive love them. When I see things with hearts on them, I want to buy those things. I rarely need them, but I usually get them because, well, HEARTS. As you know all too well, hearts are heavily associated with Valentine's Day. And I LOVE love. I really love love. This presents me with quite the predicament. Two of my favorite things in this entire world—hearts and love—are the two main marketing pieces of Valentine's Day, a day that kills me a little bit on the inside.

I do realize how silly I sound by letting a holiday that I don't even want to acknowledge make me sad (and please don't ever refer to it as Singles Awareness Day around me), but I think it's simply because it's just one more reminder that I'm still the girl who feels like a hopeless romantic because I do actually want someone to sweep me off my feet.

I *do* want to dance by the kitchen in the refrigerator light (thank you, Taylor Swift). I *do* want to kiss in the middle of a parking lot in the pouring rain after my sweet babe and I declare our love for each other. I *do* want someone to have a stash of ketchup packets handy in the event that I don't have any in my purse, and he knows that I need it when we go eat at a Tex-Mex restaurant that doesn't have any. I *do* want someone who will think that my crazy is maybe just what he needs in his life. I *do* want someone who makes my heart pound and stop at the exact same time whenever he walks into a room or says my name.

I *do* want someone to love me forever and ever, amen.

So, yes, Valentine's Day can be a little rough when I stop to think about how I'm still waiting for that man to come into my life. But I've survived 35 of those holidays already, and I can survive however many more that I have to endure. So I've made more efforts to stop throwing myself pity parties (although I would love to participate in Jessica Biel's highly memorable and inspiring piñata celebration that she and Jennifer Garner have in the movie *Valentine's Day*) and focus more on continuing to show people love as often as possible. We're all going through our own junk, and *we all need love.*

Every season of your life isn't going to be perfect or even remotely good. You will go through some that feel like unending winters full of blizzards and snow (I'm not a fan of snow and anything that makes me cold) and horrid temperatures and all of the things that feel dark and uncomfortable. But then you'll have seasons that feel like beautiful spring and summer afternoons that you could bask in forever. Regardless of what season you face, just know that you are still loved through each one, and YOU CAN DO HARD THINGS.

You can make it through a lonely holiday season. You can make it through being single when everyone around you is not. You can make it through a prolonged winter. You can make it through Valentine's Day. You can make it through the rain. (If Mariah sang it, I have to believe it.)

I hope that you remember during whatever this season is for you that you're loved just as you are and that you're never as alone as you feel.

11

When You Love You

I am about as imperfect a person as you can imagine. Some call me weird, and others say I'm quirky. I put ketchup on carrots and apple slices, and I'm not ashamed of it.

There are many qualities about me that I know aren't similar to those of other people, but I like that they make me unique. There are other things about me, though, that have been more difficult for me to accept. For instance, I've always wished that I could be prettier, and if you haven't realized by now that I really hope to fall in love and find my forever guy, then this must be the first page you've read of this book.

I'm sometimes pretty inept when it comes to men, and it's always been a trait about myself that I've seen as a monstrous flaw. I mean, I'm clearly no drama queen or anything, but I literally threw myself on the ground in my friend's office one day not too long ago when I was telling her a story of a dumb text that I sent to a guy when she had originally told me not to text him.

I'm obviously still working on loving myself through this stuff.

Just as it's so necessary that we love others, it's also extremely important that we learn to love ourselves and give ourselves some grace every once in a while. You aren't going to do everything perfectly, and you're going to have those moments when you wish you didn't do what you just did.

As someone who's been single since the first time my heart starting beating, I've learned to do pretty much everything in my life on my own. I'm fairly certain that I can even carry more grocery bags than The Rock up a few flights of stairs simply because I don't want to make multiple trips and don't have any help. I can also put together furniture and take care of various handywoman projects.

However, I sometimes forget that adulting involves a lot of responsibility and that I don't have anyone with me enough to look out for me when I mess up.

But then I'm reminded in big (and sometimes dangerous) ways.

One day when I was living by myself in an apartment in California, I somehow slept through all three of my alarms—4:09, 4:13, and 4:19 a.m. just never happened for me. When I opened my eyes at 5:17, I'm pretty sure I said my version of a cuss word (probably "shast" or "dag nabbit") and jumped out of bed. I hadn't washed my hair in about a week, and I really needed to that morning. I already knew that I didn't have time to run, but I thought about trying to squeeze in a run without touching my hair after.

For some reason that I may never know, I let hygiene win the battle that day.

I was in such a hustle to get out the door on time and was scurrying all over the place that I wasn't paying attention to much around me. I had my hands full—I decided I was going to get a pass to a gym for the day to do my tempo workout and some strength circuit training after work, so I had my shoes and change of clothes in my hands—and I bolted out of my apartment.

I actually had a really good tempo run (because that's clearly an important component of this story) and was in a much better mood than I had been (one reason why I usually prefer to run first thing in the morning). I stopped by Sprouts to get some premade meals that I could just zap in the microwave and headed home. When I lived in Dallas, I learned how to use my stove and would occasionally toss some chicken and veggies in a pan and have a nice little meal. In California, though, people—including whoever made my apartment complex—seem to prefer gas stoves. Don't ask me my opinions on gas stoves and ovens. We would be here for days.

When I walked into my apartment, the entire place reeked of gas. I hadn't used the stove or oven recently (because the one time I tried, I set off all of the smoke detectors), so I was a little confused. I looked over at the stove knobs and saw that one was slightly turned. Uh oh. I guess somehow in all of my madness of the morning I had bumped into the knob and turned it slightly—which means that gas had been filling up my apartment for a little more than 11 hours.

ADD THIS TO THE GROWING LIST OF REASONS WHY I HATE GAS-POWERED APPLIANCES.

I immediately opened my window and patio door, searched Google for what protocol was, and called the gas company to see if I was about to die. The following conversation ensued (I'm skipping the intro in which he told me to call him mister something rather than a first name and me summing up what I found when I got home and asking him more than once if I would die if I stayed there).

Mr. Guy: *Open your windows and doors, and don't turn on any appliances, including lights.*

Me: *I already did that. Wait, no appliances? But I already turned on the lights. Oh no! What will happen?!*

MG: *You turned on your lights? Was there an explosion?*

Me: *I'm still talking to you, aren't I?*

MG: *That's good. OK, don't turn on anything else.*

Me: *What about the microwave? I need to eat my dinner.*

MG: *No, don't do that. That's an appliance. Can't you leave and go grab dinner somewhere else?*

Me (replacing the meaning of "can't" with "don't want to"): *No, I can't.*

MG: *Well, I would wait at least an hour, and make sure to leave your doors open for a few hours so that the gas can dissipate.*

Me: *A few hours? It's cold outside, and that will make my apartment cold. I'm guessing I can't turn on my heater?*

MG (clearly beyond the point of minorly annoyed with me): *No, you cannot turn on your heater. Don't turn on any more appliances.*

Me: *But I need to shower.*

MG (probably wanting to reach through the phone and punch me in the face): *The shower isn't an appliance and doesn't use electricity. It's water.*

Me: *But I have to turn on another light in my bathroom to take a shower.*

MG: *Well, nothing exploded when you made the decision to turn on the first light, so you should be fine.*

Me: *I always turn on the light first thing. If there's a murderer inside, I want to see him.*

MG: *Is there anything else you need help with?*

Me: *My life.*

MG: *Anything pertaining to the gas appliances in your home?*

He had clearly reached his limit with me.

Don't tell him this, but I didn't wait the full hour to use the microwave. It's OK—nothing exploded (thanks for staying on the phone with me through that, sweet Anna J), and I didn't die from exposure to the tainted air. There's probably some scientific reason why it left my apartment pretty quickly.

Life can get messy at times, and it can be tough trying to navigate it without others to help you. I mean, what would I have done without the wise words of the guy on the phone and the people at Google? Being single isn't always challenging simply because it seems that everyone else around you has someone to hold—it can also be downright scary when you have to face situations without anyone else there with you. And I know that I'm never actually really alone, because God is always here, but there's a reason He put other people on the planet.

I hope that you surround yourself with people who remind you of the theme song from *The Wonder Years* and that you love them well. One good thing about being single—aside from being able to make new friends at the gas company because you have no clue what to do in that particular situation—is that you're still perfectly capable of loving others and being loved by others. No relationship status changes that.

And you're absolutely capable of loving yourself. I felt like a huge fool for being the reason that my apartment was full of fumes and had become a potential death trap. But I had to remind myself that I was still alive, and the whole incident had taught me a few things:

1. Slow down. You don't always have to be in a rush in everything you do.
2. Maybe my mom was smart always to triple-check that all appliances and the stove and oven were off before leaving the house, and I shouldn't have rolled my eyes at that.
3. Customer service representatives don't necessarily want to help you with your life issues outside of their scopes of expertise.

None of us really has it all together (although, if you do, can we chat so that I can have some of your insight?), and I certainly still have a lot to learn—and not just about science. But you know what? I went ahead and patted myself on the back for thinking to open the door and windows and then to call the gas company. So maybe I wasn't a complete fool after all.

I've also been trying to make sure that I encourage myself more in the other areas in my life in which I still might have some lingering insecurities. When I get that silly anxiety after sending a text to a guy I might adore and then spend way too much time overanalyzing what I sent, how long he takes to reply, and what he says back, I stop to commend myself for being brave enough to send the text in the first place.

When I look in the mirror and start to scrutinize everything that isn't super appealing reflected back at me, I try to change my way of thinking and focus on the things that I do like.

Hey, Nat, your eyes sure are a pretty shade of blue.
Your curls are totally on point—well done, sister.
Your posture has improved so much!.

As I said before, I don't think it's conceited to give yourself an uplifting pep talk, so long as you're not going around thinking and acting like you're the best gift that's ever been given to this world. I think the movie *I Feel Pretty* does a really good job of conveying this message of being able to look in the mirror and see someone who is truly beautiful rather than seeing someone who is nothing but flawed. Maybe give it a watch. I guarantee a few laughs. I watched it for the first time on a plane and laughed out loud multiple times. You're welcome, guy next to me in 7B.

We were all uniquely created and aren't meant to look or act or think just like everyone else. It's important to own and appreciate and acknowledge and embrace our distinct qualities and not be ashamed of those things that make us who we are. You are *beautifully and wonderfully made*, and nothing and no one—*not even you*—can take that away from you.

You can even write yourself a little love note or somewhat of a lunchbox note if you need a reminder.

HEYgirlHEY!

You're gorgeous. I love how intentionally you love others and truly care about them and listen to their hearts. Don't be so hard on yourself—remember that you're doing the best you can, and you deserve some grace for yourself. And don't forget, when you're making efforts to be nice to others today, show yourself some kindness and love, too.

Love,
You

12

Because Taylor Swift Songs Speak to All of the Feelings

Have you ever had a moment when you had certain expectations for a situation, but when you walked into that situation, it was almost the polar opposite of what you thought it would be?

I feel like we've all been there at some point in our lives, and sometimes those instances stay with us forever. One in particular happened to me when I was a senior in high school. My best friend and I had made a bet, and I lost. The terms of the bet required me to audition to sing at our graduation later that month.

Let's put something out there that is not only true but also a huge disappointment to the little girl who used to want to be a musical performer (albeit, those hopes were quickly dashed when I finally heard my own voice in a recording playing back to me): I am a horrible singer. Like, awful. It doesn't stop me from singing in the car (with or without others present) or performing karaoke, but it does typically hold me back from auditioning for musical theater or to sing in talent shows or to belt my heart out after all of my classmates have walked across the stage to the next chapters of their lives.

My friend thought it would be hilarious, though, to see me up on stage auditioning in front of everyone who came to watch. I didn't really care, so I picked a song that's actually a duet, and I planned to sing both parts. It was "At the Beginning" from *Anastasia*, originally performed by Donna Lewis and Richard Marx. I love that song, and I had every line memorized, and I felt like it was the perfect song for a high school graduation.

What neither of us knew, however, was that the audition didn't call for an audience—it was in a small room in front of all of the assistant principals and the choir director. I didn't think that they would find a fake audition as humorous as my peers would. So I did the only thing I could think to do when I walked into that small room in front of the panel of spectator judges: I pretended that I legitimately thought that my vocal skills were a phenomenal gift to the world.

I sang every last word of that song and even tried to sing over my own voice when both Donna and Richard are singing at the same time. It's not as easy as I imagined, but I went for it. I also tried to hit a rather high note that I definitely didn't nail. When the song ended, the APs and choir director just stared at me. You know those moments when you're so stunned by something in a bad way but don't want to say what you're really thinking because you have exactly zero words of encouragement to offer and absolutely nothing nice to say?

Yeah, it was one of those moments for them.

The worst part was that I couldn't say anything to them about the bet or the audition not being authentic. According to the stipulations of said bet, that was not allowed. I had to be convincingly real and make them believe that I genuinely thought that I was a decent enough singer to be able to perform in front of the entire study body and every single family member who came to see their adored teenagers walk across that stage for the first and last time.

It was a moment of humility that challenged me deeply at that time in my life.

That wasn't the only time I ever got myself into something that I thought would be completely different, and I know that it also won't be the last. I guess that's how life works sometimes, huh? You're constantly coming across unexpected things when you thought you knew exactly what was ahead of you. It can be humbling and daunting at times, but it can also be incredibly wonderful and freeing.

As you might imagine, I wasn't asked to sing at my high school graduation. It was for the best for everyone involved. You know what did happen, though? After that day, I realized that it actually doesn't matter what people think of me. I had already lived my life somewhat that way (with the exception of caring a bit too much about guys' opinions, of course), but that further established the longing in my heart not to live for other people and not to find my identity in them. The authority figures who had always seen me as a respectable student (even one who might talk too much at times) might have changed their opinions and seen me as crazy or a bit delusional. But that was OK. I knew that I wasn't, and that experience not only taught me to expect the unexpected as often as possible, but it also showed me that I'm capable of doing hard things, even if they bring me to levels of humility that I certainly didn't see coming.

I recently went to a karaoke bar with my sister, her husband, my parents, and some of my parents' friends. I really enjoy karaoke, but I hadn't really done it as a family affair just yet. Thankfully, I can now say that I have—my sister, my mom, and I all got up on that stage not only once but twice to belt our hearts out to Shania Twain's "Any Man of Mine" and Jon Bon Jovi's "Livin' on a Prayer." It was one of those times when you get lost in the moment and honestly forget that there are other people there because you are having so much fun with the people in your immediate circle. This typically happens when we all three get on a dance floor together, and I love being able to escape from the pressures of the world and get lost in the pure joy of being present together wherever we are and doing what we love to do.

I was highly disappointed, though, that there was absolutely no option for any Taylor Swift song. She's typically my go-to when it comes to karaoke or singing in public (I unexpectedly once performed "Love Story" for everyone at a wedding reception), and pretty much every lyric she's ever written—especially in her first few albums—can resonate with every girl who has ever breathed air.

My girl TayTay has gotten me through a lot of heartache. "All Too Well" speaks to every part of my soul, and I can feel the pain that she must have felt from the end of that relationship, even though I've never actually been in a relationship. I've had my heart broken, and I have felt all of the feelings. I listened to that song every single day on the way to work during commercial breaks of "The Musers" (a sports talk radio show on The Ticket in Dallas) in 2013 and then again in 2016. It was a painfully perfect way to start each day.

I think what I love so much about her songs and her lyrics is that they're perfectly raw and completely honest. They come from places of her heart that have experienced an array of different and sometimes contrasting emotions, and she doesn't hold back in sharing them. She reminds you of them and takes you to places that your heart needs to go to finally move toward healing. It's as if hearing someone else sing out the pain that you've gone through comforts you because it reminds you that you're not alone in what you feel—it's almost as if those feelings are validated, even though they don't need to be.

I've gone to every Taylor Swift concert (I went to the *Fearless* tour twice), and I can sing every lyric of every song by heart. I realize that I'm T-Swift bragging right now, but I can't help it. The girl just gets me.

The first time that I heard "Shake It Off," I had a lot of feelings. First of all, it was a new style of sound for Taylor, but I liked it. And the lyrics—oh, the lyrics—they really hit me. Second, I had too many things in my life that I needed to stop worrying about, and the reminder to shake off all of the things that we honestly don't need in our lives was incredibly refreshing. And, third, it simply made me want to dance. Like, a lot.

One weekend years ago, I was in a wedding (one of my many hobbies, apparently), and I did something I do at most events that have music: I made friends with the DJ. I always do this to ensure at least one T-Swizzle song gets played, and I wasn't going to start making exceptions that night. He asked me if "Shake It Off" would be alright, and I told him it would be perfect.

But I didn't realize how absolutely perfect it actually was.

When the song came on, the dance floor goers (especially the gals) became pretty enthusiastic and belted the lyrics while we all did our own versions of shaking. As I was apparently living in my own personal music video, I started thinking about some of the lyrics more, and I felt like I was letting go of the many stresses and worries that had been bogging me down. I just shook them all off and left them there on that dance floor where they belonged.

One of my favorite parts of the song is when she mentions dancing on her own and making up her own moves as she goes. You see, I dance on my own the majority of the time, and I never know what move to expect next. I just kind of go with it, and I think it's a good way to approach life in some ways. You might be dancing on your own, but it can be a beautiful dance—even if those around you don't think the moves are so lovely. It's your dance, not theirs.

The entire song is such a great reminder of why we shouldn't be so focused on how other people perceive us. Even when it comes to relationships. Excuse my middle-school-sounding wording, but if a guy doesn't like me back, I'm just going to shake it off. I was thinking about this as I was likely looking like a flailing bird when my friends Maddie and Whitney finally joined me on the dance floor (I had told them to be there for this song). We all kept letting ourselves be completely carefree as the perfect anthem continued, and I felt so much better at the end of it. I felt free.

Then I thought of "Shake It Off" during a worship song at church that Sunday. (Yes, you read that correctly.)

We were singing "In Christ Alone," and some of the lyrics stood out to me more than they usually do, especially the words that speak of not letting the actions or plots of others take you away from Him—because you're standing in His power. That moment brought me back to the chorus of Taylor Swift's song, when she sings about how people are going to do the things they do, regardless of how those actions impact you. And that's when you simply "shake it off."

Because you can have a say in how the words and actions of others impact your heart and what you think of yourself.

Just like in the worship song: People and things are going to try to lead you away from the Lord, but all you have to do is shake all of those things off and keep your feet firmly planted on His solid ground.

Whether it's people or situations, you're going to face difficult things in life, but that doesn't mean that you have to be defeated by them. People aren't always going to be nice—shake it off, and give them grace. Your heart might be broken—shake it off, and look forward to new beginnings. People may lie or deceive you in various ways—shake it off, and put your trust in what is genuine. Life is going to throw you curves—shake it off, and keep swinging for the fences.

And you might find that others will want to join you in dancing to "this.sick.beat."

SECTION 3

YOU MATTER

13

When You See People for Their Hearts

When I first moved out to California in 2017, one thing I noticed immediately is that people in California and people in Texas are different—like, a lot different. That's not necessarily a bad thing, but it does mean that it will take a person going from one state to the other a little bit of time to get used to the fact that she can't have the same expectations for everyone.

I love Texas with all of my heart, and it was really difficult to leave it without knowing how long I'd be gone or if I would ever live here again. During my first few weeks in Southern California, I became aware that people weren't talking to me as much as I was used to. Like when I would go to the grocery store, other customers wouldn't always say "hello" or flash welcoming smiles when we made eye contact—if they made eye contact at all. When I went running, each person I passed wouldn't greet me with a "good morning" or other form of salutation. At first, I thought maybe people on the West Coast just weren't as friendly.

And then I had to check my own heart.

What I discovered was that, while I didn't necessarily receive the initial openness with which I had become all too familiar, once I started talking to them and actually getting to know them, the people in California were just as warm and genuine as anyone else I'd met. It just meant that I might have to be the one initiating conversations much of the time—and, let's be honest here, I'm completely OK with that. Talking to people is one of my favorite pastimes.

When I was younger (especially before I knew Jesus), I probably judged people quite a bit. I'm not going to bring up middle school and those horrible years yet again (even though I sort of just did), but I guarantee that I probably thought and said a lot of things about other people that I definitely shouldn't have thought and said. As I've gotten older and tried to live what I believe, I've tried to love people well. But that doesn't mean that it has always been easy not to judge them. We live in a comparison culture, and it can be tough sometimes not to let judgments enter our minds when we see people looking or living differently than we look and live.

During the time I lived in SoCal, though, God did so many things in my life and in my heart that changed the way I see people. Suddenly judgment isn't really a thing anymore. I'm not lying when I say that, if we ever meet each other, I promise to accept you as you are and not judge you for anything—not your clothes, not your appearance, not the way you talk, not the way you live your life, not your past, not your present, not what you hope for the future. Nothing. I'm not better than anyone, and I'm not going to pretend that I know how to live your life better than you do.

I've come to a much deeper understanding that we're all uniquely different, and we all have different stories and means to get to where we're supposed to go. My way isn't necessarily the best way for you, and your way likely won't be the right way for me. Our different choices and different paths and different lifestyles and different hair and different fashion senses and different anything and everything aren't bad—*they're simply different.*

And, no matter how different we are, we are all still valued, we are all still loved, and *we all still matter.*

It's humbling to realize that you haven't been loving people as well as you should have because you weren't fully accepting them for who they already are. We all have junk and stuff from our pasts that we might wish weren't actually part of our pasts. We all have moments we wish we could take back. We all have our own passions and desires. We all have our own choices to make and hobbies we enjoy. And we don't have to be ashamed to be the people we are simply because we're afraid of what other people might think.

OK, so I guess that I am going to bring up middle school again. Back in that ugly era of my life, I wore a lot of Tommy Hilfiger collared shirts because those were the latest trend. In all honesty, I hate collared shirts. Like, utterly detest them. I think they look great on other people, but I'm not a fan of how I look or feel in them, so I never wear them now. But I wore them back then to fit in with everyone else.

At some point, I stopped caring about that kind of stuff and started wearing whatever I want to wear. I truly believe that any colors go together, and I'm not concerned with other people's perceptions of my attire.

I also had to stop caring about what people think of what I do. I love dental hygiene in an almost obsessive kind of way. I'm one of those people who flosses and brushes after every meal and after every snack, too. It doesn't matter where I am—I will brush my teeth if I'm not near a sink or restroom and won't be for a while. I've brushed my teeth while walking in downtown San Diego. I brush my teeth in my car. I've brushed my teeth at the table at the froyo place because I was chatting with my friend and didn't want to interrupt our convo to have to go to the restroom to do so. I've brushed my teeth at the airport when the bathroom was really far, and I knew I'd have to walk there later, anyway, to use the restroom before my flight. I've brushed my teeth in a lot of places, and I've gotten a lot of looks from people. I've caught a few people taking pictures and videos and maybe sending them to friends or posting them somewhere.

(Side note: I almost took out the part about me brushing my teeth at the froyo table because I know that a lot of people would see that as impolite, but then I remembered the entire point of this chapter and left it in here. After all, this is the real me, people.)

Here's the truth: Even though people may frown upon it or think that it's really bad manners, brushing my teeth in public places doesn't change my heart or my character in any way, no matter how many people judge me for it.

I think it's important to change our mindsets when it comes to how we view people—we need to see them for their hearts and with our hearts and not with merely our eyes. Let's be perfectly real here—we're all complete messes. Even the people who look like they have it all together have their issues that they don't want the entire world to see or that might cause others to think less of them.

I'll never forget something that my friend Bonnie said to me years ago after a coworker had made a rather insulting comment about my outfit: "The world would be a better place if people would stop judging."

Amen, sister.

For many of us, as we get older, we tend to care less and less about what people think of us in some areas of our lives—we'll go to the grocery store in pajamas, and we'll say things out loud in public that might have embarrassed us 13 years ago. But, even as adults, every once in a while, other people can still make us feel small.

People are always going to judge us. It doesn't mean that it's right, but it's a reality. We don't have to let their opinions impact the way we live, though. We are the unique individuals we are for reasons, and we don't need to change simply because of what others might think about us. If you want to sing Whitney or Britney at karaoke, please belt it. If you want to veer away from tradition when planning your wedding, go for it. If you want to believe that leggings are pants (because they are), believe it, and wear them with pride—and I will support you and wear them right along with you. If you want to put ketchup instead of mustard on your hot dog, slather away. If you really like the shirt that your friend said she'd never wear in public, for the love, buy the shirt. If you are sitting at the airport and realize you forgot to put on deodorant, but the bathroom is too far away, and the deodorant is right in your bag and would be easier to put on right where you are, you do what you need to do, regardless of the looks you receive.

Just be you.

Bonnie was right: The world would absolutely be a better place if people would stop judging. But it would also be better if we stopped caring so much about those judgments. It's a continual process for me, but I have to remind myself more and more to be me all of the time, even when it comes to any guy who captivates my attention. After all, he should accept me for who I am—just like others should accept you for the person you are. And, to be honest, the people who truly care about you won't make you feel like you're not good enough as you are.

Because you truly do matter, and love is bigger and better than any person's judgment could ever be.

14

Because You're Worth the Fight

There are many things of which I'm not completely certain in life—why California insists on charging for grocery store bags and an extra 10 cents (or something ridiculous like that) per water bottle, why more people don't use emojis when they text, how you're expected to get a job when you have no experience when all companies want is to hire people with experience, how the mind of a man works, and why Chick-fil-A seems to think "a handful of Chick-fil-A sauce" means two sauces.

But I am certain of this: Love is bigger and more powerful than we could ever imagine.

Sometimes I wonder why I still believe in love stories. Sure, I've seen enough romcoms to fill up an entire heart with dreams and hopes of what I think my own love story should or might look like, but for a while I thought that I haven't come close enough to a love story of my own for me to have much hope left. I don't want that to sound too dramatic or pessimistic, but it often felt like a lofty daydream that will never actually be a reality for me. And it's not like I can even become that "crazy cat lady" person because it turns out that I'm actually allergic to cats, and I'm not even a big animal person, anyway.

For years, I've tried to fill my time with so many things so that I don't have time to think about the fact that I'm alone, and a lot of these time fillers end up allowing me to be around people for enough time that my alone time is actually very welcomed. The problem with that, though, is that I usually end up piling way too much on my plate and wind up more stressed than any one human should be. I've started going to nail salons almost once a week to receive 20-minute neck/shoulder massages because they only charge $1 per minute, and those ladies really know how to work my knots out—but it's a little ridiculous for one gal to have *that* much tension.

I used to joke with my friends in high school about me never having a boyfriend, and those jokes carried on into college and then into my early 20s. And then it reached a point when it didn't seem much like a joke that would make anyone laugh anymore but more of one that made me feel like *I* was the joke. I felt like that for a long time, actually, and it wasn't super easy to get past that feeling. I watched friend after friend get engaged, and I stood by them on their wedding days, and it started to hurt a little more inside each time knowing that I couldn't even look out into the crowds of people and have someone looking and smiling only at me.

I've never let myself imagine what I want my wedding to be like because I know there's a real possibility that it will never happen. Plus, I don't want to get caught up in wanting a wedding more than a marriage—I want the real deal. I want a man who loves me forever and wants to stand by me through everything this life throws our way. I don't care about the colors of dresses or what flowers are placed where (now that I think about it, I actually don't even want flowers at a potential wedding because I don't care for them). I only care that I actually have someone who wants nothing more than for me to walk down the aisle only to him and him forever.

Maybe you've already found your true love, and y'all are continuing to write your forever love story together. I hope that I get to hear about it someday. Or maybe you're more like me and are still waiting and hoping for the person who's going to complete that love story with you. While there's nothing wrong with keeping that hope alive, please don't let it stop you from still living and writing your own story. Whether you end up doing life with someone right by your side or taking more of a solo route, *your story and what you do still matter*. No one person makes you worth any more or any less than you already are—you *matter* on your own.

And if you're going through a heartache or really difficult time right now that makes you not believe any of what I said is true, believe me when I say that I know that it's tough. I know that it hurts. I know that there are so many moments when you want to crawl into a corner away from everybody else in the rest of the world and just sob until there aren't any more tears left to stream down your blotchy cheeks. I know that it feels like it's never going to stop hurting, and your broken heart will never be pieced back together. I know that it seems like there isn't anyone else on the entire planet who will ever make you feel the way he made you feel. I know that you don't want to give him up. I know that all of the memories are incredibly wonderful and incredibly painful at the same time. I know that it feels like you will never be loved by anyone.

I know how you feel, sister. I've been there, too.

And I promise you that *it does get better*.

You are a lot stronger than you know. You don't have to believe me now, but you'll eventually realize it. You're so much more capable of picking yourself up and pressing on than you think. And you don't have to try to do it all on your own—in fact, I don't recommend that. Is it trite to tell you to pray about it? Probably. But I do think that you should pray about it. You may not magically be healed of your heartache the instant you utter the words in your heart, but your prayers will be heard, and your God will be there with you every step of the way.

I've dealt with kidney stone issues for years, and those suckers are painful. I once had one that was 9 millimeters in diameter (the average size of a kidney stone is 3–4 millimeters) that got stuck in my ureter, and I had to have two surgeries for it (the first surgery failed). This was in the same year I had had a surgery for my other kidney months before, and that surgery had resulted in a kidney infection. Needless to say, I had a great deal of physical pain that year.

But you know what? The broken heart I was going through at that time hurt so much worse.

There's something about a heart that's been shattered that causes this inexplicable pain that's pretty incomparable to anything. It's almost like it causes actual physical pain at the same time it's causing all of these emotion-wrenching feelings that seem to transform your world entirely. It can really suck the life out of you, leaving you feeling weak and hopeless and often pretty apathetic. You feel emotions that you didn't even know existed, and you're amazed at how your eyes could still have any tears left unshed after the enormous amount you've already cried.

But a broken heart can't completely break you if you don't let it.

We often have to go through the tough times to be the people we're meant to be and to go the places we're meant to go. If I hadn't gone through such a tough time when I did, I might not have moved to California in 2017. I can tell you right now that that move didn't just change my life for the obvious reasons of moving across the country—*it changed me* and helped me realize what I was truly supposed to be pursuing in life.

It's OK to wallow. It's actually probably healthy to. I mean, Lorelai Gilmore was a huge advocate of it, and she's a sage to be trusted. But after you've done whatever is the best amount of wallowing for you, look in the mirror, and remind yourself that you're a dazzling and remarkable woman who is capable of making your mark on the world simply by being who you were always meant to be and that you don't need a man. Sure, you may want one, and you may very well end up with one, but you don't actually *need* one. *You're enough.*

So let that broken heart mend, and let yourself believe that you will love again—because love is worth it, and *you are worth it*.

Remember that gun situation I mentioned earlier? When that man showed me his gun, and I realized that my life was in danger,

I took off running. I ran as fast as I've probably ever run before, and I started going in a zig-zag pattern so that I'd at least be a moving target. In that moment, *I fought for myself.*

And you should, too.

You're worth taking chances and doing the things that might make you a little queasy. You're worth letting your heart feel deeply and love intentionally. You're worth pursuing the passions that set your heart into motion. You're worth running full force ahead toward your dreams. You're worth the investment of time and energy. You're worth being loved.

And you're worth fighting for yourself.

15

When Your Identity Isn't Found in What You Do

I love running. I'm not sure if that's always been the case, but it's always been a part of my life. I started playing soccer at a very young age (although I mainly joined to be like my brother and for the Gatorade at halftime) and continued to play for 15 years. I played forward and midfield, which involved quite a bit of running, and I always enjoyed going back and forth and up and down the field, trying to outrun the defenders to the ball and take it past them to score.

My dad also used to make us run. I remember this one house that had an extravagant display of Christmas decorations that caused cars to line up down the entire street to see. The owner of the home was the guy who was the head of MJ Designs (the company that later became Michael's) at the time, and he seemed to delight in making sure that the kids in our town enjoyed holidays like Christmas and Halloween (he always gave out king-sized candy bars). His neighborhood was not too far from where we lived, and I can think of at least one year when my dad made us run there so that we didn't have to wait in the line of cars.

I remember the air feeling really cold in my lungs, but my dad told me that it was good for me, and so I didn't stop to walk when the physical pain set in.

I ran cross country and track in high school, but I wasn't bringing home tons of medals or filling up trophy cases, and it wasn't until I was in my 20s that I became more passionate about running and started being more competitive each time I stepped on the line. In early 2010, I began running with a faster group of people in the Dallas running community. At first, I was pretty intimidated—I knew who they all were (speedy people are pretty well-known in the Big D), and I knew that they were all capable of going much faster paces than I ever could.

In time, they helped me to become a stronger runner, and I even gained a few of my best friends from this group. Sometimes when we develop talents and passions, though, we allow ourselves to be consumed by them and to let those things define us. For me, that became the case with my running.

It got pretty bad, even to the point that I finally recognized that I cared way too much about my performance. It wasn't even what other people thought of me or how fast I was that mattered—*I was afraid to fail and to disappoint myself.* I had always excelled in sports, and it never even occurred to me that I had let myself find my identity in them. I was always the athletic one growing up. I needed to be the best in order for me to feel like I was good enough, and I carried that with me into my adulthood as I continued to run road races. I wanted every single race to be faster than my last, which is honestly an unrealistic expectation.

It was not healthy by any means.

I'll never forget one weekend when I went on a women's retreat with my church, and I introduced myself to someone I hadn't met before. She seemed to recognize me somewhat, and when she heard my name, she said "oh, you're the runner!" I said the first thing that popped into my head without even thinking about what was coming out of my mouth.

"Yeah, but I'm so much more than that."

And I was right. It had finally hit me that I wasn't just a runner. Sure, it was something that I loved to do, but it wasn't all of who I was. While I would love to be able to run forever and whenever I want, it's also something that can be fleeting at times, and it can be taken away from me—which it was for a while.

When I say I used to race, I mean, like, a lot. I think there was one year when I ran at least one road race a month, and three or four of those races were half marathons. I can't fully explain it, but there was something about racing that caused me anxiety in a good way yet also helped grow my confidence in a number of ways, as well.

Then 2017 happened.

At the end of 2016, I started to have weird (and pretty much constant) internal pain and frequently had blood in my urine. I had been training for the half marathon that I ran every December in Dallas, and I was excited for it because I felt more confident than ever going into that race. But around Thanksgiving that year, that pain I'd been having escalated. I ran the eight-mile Turkey Trot and didn't do as well as I'd hoped, and a large reason for that was because I was in extreme pain the entire race.

When I woke up the morning of the half marathon a few weeks later, I could barely walk and knew the race was out of the question. I eventually went to multiple doctors, and months went on before it was finally determined that I needed to have kidney surgery. I had a total of three kidney surgeries in 2017, which meant that the idea of racing was not even a thought that crossed my mind. There were quite a few periods of time that year when I was thankful if I was even able to run at all—it's certainly not easy or pleasant when you have a stent in you.

It's been a tough journey since then, and it's not like those surgeries ended all of my issues with kidney stones. Though I've been able to train much more than I did that year, I took a very long time off from racing, and the thought of getting back out there made me more nervous than I knew I could be when it came to competing.

Even as I'm writing this, I still haven't lined up on that starting line, and I'm trying not to feel queasy thinking about it.

My dear friend Amanda and I were talking about this the one day and why I feel such a need to do well when I race. Aside from the fact that I'm a competitive person, why is it so important for me to feel accomplished when I cross the finish line? We talked about it for a bit, and it definitely runs deeper than simply wanting to win or achieve my goals.

I started thinking about this more later that day, and it became pretty clear: In the past, I let winning races or running fast times make me feel like I was enough. There are more than a few areas of my life in which I don't always feel like I'm adequate—I had a really rough time in college and trying to figure out where I belonged; I've had multiple careers and haven't always felt like I've excelled in them; I'm 35 and got my first ever passport when I was 34 (and I still don't have any stamps in it); I've never been in a relationship, which certainly makes me feel like a failure in more ways than one; and the list continues. But when I crossed those finish lines and had accomplished what I set out to accomplish, I was good enough. When I didn't, I wasn't.

My friends, I was once again in a tangled web of lies.

It's great to have goals and passions and to pursue those goals and passions, but it's also good to realize that you aren't going to hit the bullseye every single time you aim for it. One day when I was at work when I lived in California, I cut a tag out of the side of the inside of my dress because it was really bothering my leg. But when I cut it, it was even pokier and worse. So I cut it where it was threaded in, and the next thing I knew, there was a hole in the side of my dress. I don't have an emergency sewing kit (and, even if I did, I wouldn't know how to use it), so I stapled my dress. I also spilled a large amount of water—not once but twice—all down the front of that same dress on that very same day. And those were the good things that happened that day. Obviously, I was killin' it in life. But I survived the day, and I wasn't less of a person because of it, just like I won't be less of a person if I run a race and am slower than I want to be.

Here's the thing: It doesn't matter how many races I've won. It doesn't matter how successful I've been in my career. It doesn't matter how many dresses I've ripped holes in trying to cut out tags. It doesn't matter how many staples I've used trying to patch them back up. It doesn't matter how many dates I've had. It doesn't matter how many guys have looked my way. None of those things holds value in my worth. I can't let deferred hopes or unattained goals make me feel like I'm not good enough.

Because I am enough—just as I am. I was made in the image of Christ, and I don't have to be someone else or put a bunch of W's in the win column. I don't have to pursue this type of perfection that I'm never going to obtain. I'm going to lose. I'm going to rip clothes. I'm going to have my heart broken. It's just part of life.

But it doesn't change my worth.

I might be in love with Brett Eldredge. I've always loved his music, but I saw him in concert at the OC Fair in 2018, and I fell hard for him. He has a song called "Somethin' I'm Good At," and he mentions a ton of things that aren't really parts of his skillset, but he is able to love well and put a smile on the face of the girl in the song who has captured his heart. I'd like to be like that—if I fail at all other things in this world, I would like to be able to love people well. I won't always be capable of doing everything I want in life, but I can always show love to others. We all can. **People need love, and they need to know that they are enough.**

And so do you.

16

Because Wearing Pink on Wednesdays Is Actually Meaningful

On Wednesdays, I wear pink.

Yes, this was originally inspired by the movie *Mean Girls*. In my third or fourth year as a high school teacher, I started a "On Tuesdays, we wear side braids" thing, but then some of my students and I decided that we should follow suit with the movie and wear pink every Wednesday. It was a fun way for us to have something to look forward to each week, and I like to think that it created a stronger bond between all of us.

I took this tradition with me to the corporate world when I transitioned out of teaching in 2015. Some of the people at my new financial services firm were a little hesitant at first, but I later had lots of people—including many of the guys—participating. It brought my heart such tremendous joy.

I had even gotten the president of our company on board, and he told me that pink is actually the color of gratitude, which made me love the idea of wearing this color at least once a week even more. Wednesday is the middle of the week, which seems like the perfect time to me to remind yourself of the reasons you have to be thankful. Pink isn't even my favorite color (it's seafoam green and an aqua-ish turquoise blue), but I wear it every single Wednesday, and it helps to remind me that, even when I have things that make me want to wallow, I also have plenty of reasons to be thankful.

In the last job that I had in California, I became good friends with three other women in the office, and we started weekly Wednesday gratitude emails. Even after one of the girls left, and then I left, we have still kept that weekly email going, and my heart does a little happy dance every Wednesday when I send out that email and get their replies with bullet-point lists of things that are going on in our lives that give us reasons to be thankful. We talk about the big things in life as well as the small, and it helps to connect our hearts even more in spite of the many miles between us.

I know that I'm not skilled at everything I attempt, as I've already told you, but I try to remind myself to be grateful for the gifts and passions that I do have that I'm able to use to help and inspire others. I would encourage you to acknowledge the things you're really great at in your own life and continue to pursue them and encourage yourself along the way.

You're going to have those "off" days, and you're going to have moments when you wish you had certain talents and abilities that you don't. There's no getting around it—life is just tough sometimes. But, rather than focusing on everything you can't do or don't do well, focus on the things that light fires in your soul, and continue to do those things that you do really well—and do them often. You have those gifts and talents for a reason, and they're meant to be used, not overshadowed by all of the flaws that you think you have.

I'm single and, thus far, seem to have lacked the ability to attract the guys I like for long enough for them to stick around or pursue me, but I'm really good at encouraging people and leading them, and that's what I'm going to focus on right now. It's OK that I don't have a boyfriend or husband; I have a community of people I love and trust and am excited for what's possibly ahead. I don't need to worry or stress about the things that I don't have—I'd rather pay more attention to the gifts I've been given. In those moments when

I think I don't have love, I'm going to remind myself that I'm able to love and be loved in bigger ways than my mind can fathom.

I hope that you know how special you are as you are, and I hope that you're able to focus on the unique things that make you who you are, and I hope you let them shine as brightly as light from the sun when you first walk outside after being in a dark movie theater.

Because light will always beat the dark shadows that try to ruin it.

I also encourage you to find other aspects of your life that bring you sparks of joy, even if they're less evident things that often get overlooked. You know, like fruit punch Jolly Ranchers.

The month of November always reminds us that we need to be thankful. In reality, it would be great if we could express our gratitude about more things in life much more often than only one month out of the year—like maybe on Wednesdays when you join me in wearing pink. It's probably really good for our well-beings. I'm no doctor or psychologist, but I'm pretty sure that's accurate.

I honestly think it's important to remind yourself that there are wonderful aspects of life that often arrive without huge grandeur or obviousness. I'm not the best about doing this. Sometimes I let the big things in my life—both positive and negative—overshadow what my focus should really be on: little pieces of joy.

I've compiled a short list of thank-you notes to shine spotlights on those important bits of greatness.

SportsCenter — Truthfully, I don't know what I would do without you, *SC*. Sadly, I cannot always watch every single game played in every single sport, but you make that OK. You let me know what happened, and you make me smile by bringing in some pretty witty anchors to deliver it all (I'm looking at you, Neil and Stan). I start my morning with you, and I end my day with you. *Thank you.*

The treadmill — Let's be honest: Most of the time, I say that I don't like you. But that's not very kind of me, because you really do come in handy when it's lightning outside or on those very rare days when it ices in Texas in the winter months. Where would I run on those days if it weren't for you? Through the halls of my apartment complex? No. That would wake up my neighbors. But you don't wake up my neighbors, and that's an admirable quality. *Thank you.*

My personal space heater — The offices I've worked in always felt like what I imagine living in an actual refrigerator would feel like. It's almost like the episode of *I Love Lucy* when she gets trapped in a freezer. (There is zero exaggeration here.) But you changed that. You made it close to 80 degrees all of the time at my desk, and now you provide extra warmth in my apartment during the winter months. Without you, I would probably have lips bluer than those of Kate Winslet when she's telling Leo DiCaprio that she'll never let go (there was room on that door, Rose). You're an actual life saver. *Thank you.*

The Musers — Fellas, my drive to work in the morning could be so boring, but it's the opposite. Your observations and fake interviews always fill my mornings with laughter and happiness. I never thought I would be entertained by something like a pretend station mouse with a high-pitched giggle (or admit to it), but for some reason I am. Please never stop talking. *Thank you.*

Scarves — I hate cold weather. I normally don't like to use the word "hate," but I mean it in every sense of the word right now. I hate it. But you help provide me warmth. I cannot effectively tell you how much you mean to me, but you are part of the reason I survive the colder air. You come in so many colors and styles, and you match with anything (because anything matches if you wear it with confidence). *Thank you.*

Genuine people — You know what it means to be honest and care about how you treat others. You say you're going to do something, and you actually follow through with it. Others appreciate that. Hearts matter to you, because people matter to you. *Thank you.*

Wheat Thins — I honestly can't find fitting words to describe the joy you bring to my life. You've been there for me in every single season at every single meal. You cure my hunger pangs so that the world doesn't have to suffer from my hanger BECAUSE IT IS SO REAL. I will love you until the day I die. If I ever develop a gluten allergy, I will choose death or horrible cases of stomach issues over giving you up. Just like Toni Braxton once poetically sang (regarding a man, though, not crackers), you mean the world to me, my sweet Wheat Thins, and I'm pretty sure that I sometimes feel like you are my everything.

During one of my years of teaching, I used to take my favorite class outside every once in a while on nice days, and we would sit in a circle and go around and share highs and lows of our weeks. I was really thankful during those moments, and I think the kids were, too. It forced each one of us to find at least one positive thing going on in our lives to share for the highs, and it felt good.

Because being thankful feels good.

Life is hard. There's no way around that. There's a saying about learning to dance in the rain, and maybe being grateful for the "little" (I think they're actually really big) things in life is doing just that. Maybe it will help during the tough times to remind others how thankful you are for them—because they matter. And you matter. And being grateful matters.

Because, to me, thankfulness is another way to spread love that's so badly needed in this world.

When You Let Your Heart Feel

I think it's important to be open and genuine, and sometimes that involves sharing your heart and being vulnerable when you might not want to.

As I've mentioned probably more times than any human wants to hear thus far, sometimes it's really tough being single when you're an adult. Even if it's not necessarily true, it seems like every other human being around you is in a relationship and has his or her person to do life with and make memories together. And plenty of people you don't even ask have their opinions regarding what you should or shouldn't do to make sure that you don't spend the rest of your life singing the catchy Farmers Only jingle.

And apparently others can tell that you're single without you telling them. I bought a sofa a couple of years ago (well, it's really a loveseat, but they're all the same to me). I had been watching television while sitting on a blowup mattress, and that lifestyle was getting old and uncomfortable, so it was time for something else. When I told the guy who sold it to me that I thought the loveseat was a better option than the full-sized sofa for me, he said this: "Yeah, it's the perfect size for someone who's alone."

Maybe I have a vibe about me or something.

I've also mentioned previously that, while I've never actually had a boyfriend or even been in an actual relationship, I've had my heart broken. And, for a long while not too long ago, I felt like I was going through a never-ending heartache that I couldn't seem to escape, no matter what I did. Honestly, I still feel those unwanted pangs every now and then. Unfortunately, there's no timetable for mending a broken heart—we're all so different, and we all handle our pain in different ways.

For me, I've always tried to deal with emotional pain the same way I deal with physical pain: I ignore it. I do this for as long as possible, and then I usually reach a point when I have to face the fact that the pain is actually there, and there's no way to pretend it's not there anymore—I simply have to acknowledge it.

It had been almost two years since my heart was ripped out of my chest, thrown to the ground, smashed into thousands of tiny little pieces, and then stomped all over by the guy who walked away from it. (There's no such a thing as being overly dramatic or exaggerating things when it comes to a broken heart, right?) I thought that I would have gotten over it more quickly than I did, but for a long time I simply tried to mask the pain that was still prevalent for far longer than I ever expected. It hurt for a while, and I missed him, which made me feel foolish and pathetic.

But I also know that I was neither foolish nor pathetic—I was simply a girl who cared about a boy who didn't care about her. It wasn't exactly the classic romance tale, but it was my reality for what felt like a rather lengthy amount of time.

One evening when I was living in California, I went to a panel discussion at a church that was somewhat connected with mine, and the topic was about dating in today's society. It was kind of difficult to take advice from the married couples up there (especially the ones who had been married for 20 years and more), and I wish they would have had more than one single person to share some insight, but I ended up having a rather enlightening moment on my own in the midst of it all.

As I was listening to some of the couples share their stories of how they met, I began to feel alone and a little sad. I hadn't cried in a while, and I had a feeling that the waterworks were coming soon. (Part of that not-acknowledging-my-emotional-pain thing that I do means that I ignore moments when I want to cry, so I end up bottling up a ton of emotions, and they typically come pouring out all at once when I least expect them to.) I did the only thing that ever makes sense to me when everything around me makes zero sense: I started praying.

God knows my heart, and I began unloading it in a prayer of brokenness, asking Him what I was supposed to do. *I hate the online stuff—it's not part of my story, and I know it. But I'm hurting, and I'm still sad about [him]. God, if I'm supposed to be single forever, can you please take away this desire in my heart? And, regardless, can you please take away my feelings for him? Am I ever going to meet my person? What do I do, Lord?*

And then I heard this quiet, calming voice that has spoken truth to me so many times: *Don't you trust me? I've never let you down.*

Talk about a sucker punch to the gut. This big and powerful God who has the entire world in His hands—the One who called me out to California and has always provided for me in more ways than I could ever have imagined—*truly cares* about me and has a plan that is more perfect than anything that I could ever create. Like the song "Oceans" reminds me, He's never failed me, and He won't start now. That doesn't mean that I'm going to walk into an elevator tomorrow and meet the man of my dreams, but it does mean that, whether or not I do ended up falling in love with the one guy who picks me out of every other girl in the world, He's got big plans for me.

And I *do* trust Him.

We sang two songs in church that following Sunday that both had lines about God never failing us and never letting us down. And when I looked up, the lights above the stage changed colors to seafoam green and aqua-ish turquoise blue—my two favorite colors. To this day, I still don't know if I imagined that happening or if it actually did, but it truly doesn't matter. I think it was His way of reminding me that He is who He says He is, He's always present in my life, and He's taking care of the things that cause me worry and anxiety—He's funny like that.

~ ~

I can't always explain the feelings in my heart and the things it leads me to do, but I do know that I trust it.

And that I need to let it express those feelings more.

I consider myself a fairly intelligent person, but there are definitely times when I don't really do that whole "thinking" thing. It's happened before that I've been at a restaurant and using one of those old-school ketchup bottles that you have to hit to get the actual ketchup out. After I did, some ketchup kind of dripped out on the side of the mouth of the bottle, and I licked it off. Yes, I licked a restaurant's ketchup bottle. I wasn't thinking—I just did it. By the time I realized what I was doing, it was far too late.

There are quite a few other areas of my life in which I don't really let my brain be in charge. I'm more of the heart-thinker type. When I know in my heart that I'm supposed to do something, I typically don't give it much thought—I just do it.

Nike has clearly gotten the best of me.

While I use my heart for both big and little decisions, I don't always do the best job of letting it feel and express all of the emotions that it needs to. Going back to that point about me being a bottler in that regard and how it's a disaster when I actually let my tear ducts do their job—cue an unexpected sob situation.

It was a Tuesday, and I thought it was just a normal day, but it was apparently actually a day for the waterworks. My author hero Annie Downs always says "Tuesday, you ain't cute," and maybe she's on to something there. (I usually feel sorry for Tuesday, though—it's such an overlooked day. Also, I was born on a Tuesday, so I guess I can't really refer to it as not cute and feel good about that.) It was October at the time (exactly a week before my 34th birthday), and I think it had been since January or February since I'd cried, so I guess it was time. As usual when this happens, I was not expecting it—it just happened. We had a night of prayer and worship at my church, and my heart started to feel heavy on the drive over there. When I got inside, I began to notice that my eyes and their rusty tear ducts were weakening. I warned my friend Amanda that I felt like I was on the verge of crying but that I thought I would be able to hold it back.

Like Lloyd Christmas, I was way off.

I was holding it together until we started singing "Do It Again," a song I love with my whole heart with lyrics that get me at the very core. The first three lines played, and I lost it. They talk about feeling like the walls around you should have fallen by now, but God isn't one to fail us—ever.

I think the weight of the truth and power behind the lyrics hit me hard. I immediately bolted out of the room and into a corner in an empty hallway so that I could sit on the ground and begin what became ugly convulsive sobbing. I couldn't stop. I tried. I failed. The tears had started, and they weren't letting up anytime soon. I finally gave up trying to stop and just let the crying and all of the feelings consume all of me. It was exhausting.

By the time the song ended, that sweet Amanda was sitting on the floor next to me with her arm wrapped around me. She didn't need to say anything for a while—she just let me let out the emotions that had been in hiding for too long. Then she prayed with me, and we chatted a little before rejoining everyone else.

Later that week, I was running and thinking about a lot of different things, particularly how quickly life happens and how every single event and moment we face has purpose for the places we're supposed to go, the things we're supposed to do, and the people we're supposed to be. I reflected on a rather painful time a couple of years ago that deeply impacted me. And then I did something I've never actually done before: I thought about every single emotion I felt during that time and even after, and I let myself *actually feel* those things. I didn't cry or stop running or have any outward showing of anything—I simply let my heart do what it does best.

I let my heart think for me.

We all have different ways of processing and expressing our emotions, and I'm not expecting a monumental change for me anytime soon. I'm not perfect by any means (after all, I did lick a ketchup bottle that's the property of a restaurant where people other than just me eat), and I'm honestly still trying to figure out this whole "life" thing. But one thing I realized on that run was that, while I may not normally know how to deal with my emotions, there's one thing that my heart feels that I know what to do with: love. It's not simply an emotion or action—it's so much more that I'm not even sure there's an accurate word to describe exactly what it is, other than it's what God is and what God does.

But I do know that we're all capable of it.

Maybe you're like me and don't cry very often. Or maybe you're the type of person who cries merely from hearing the theme song of *This Is Us*. And I'm sure that there's a balance in there somewhere, too. Regardless, I know that it's OK to let yourself feel. It's OK to let yourself cry. (Yes, this is a slight pep talk to myself, too.) It's OK to hurt and laugh and mourn and rejoice and ache and smile and let every other feeling be one that you acknowledge in a healthy way, even if that includes throwing rocks at a building or breaking plates and hitting things with a baseball bat at a place called The Anger Room. But, most of all, it's OK to let your heart love.

Because that's the most important heart thing of them all.

I don't know what you're going through in life. Maybe you're searching for something you can't seem to find. Maybe you're hurting and in need of genuine love. Maybe you're lonely and feel like you're unlovable. Whatever the case may be, I hope that you don't believe the lies, and I hope that you don't lose hope. I hope that you keep pressing on through the storms of heartache that try to knock you down. I hope that you know that you are worthy and enough with or without someone else standing by your side.

And I hope that you know that you are loved by the One who will love you more than anyone else in the entire world ever could.

Because People Can Change Our Lives and Not Even Know It

Every once in a while, people come into your life and change it in more ways than you ever could have imagined.

And those people may have no clue how much they impacted you.

As I've mentioned, more than three years ago, the pain of a broken heart that I thought was never going to heal began. Maybe I should have seen it coming; maybe there was no way for me to know. Either way, it happened, and it hurt. A lot.

Right around that same time, though, this tiny human entered the world—sweet Olivia, the precious little girl who made me an aunt for the very first time. As soon as I saw her and held that angelic little body in my arms, I was smitten. Little did I know, this precious gift would walk alongside me through a dark season that was filled with more crying than just her baby tears.

From the day she was born, I committed to be a big part of her life, and I certainly wanted her as part of mine. I went over to my brother's and sister-in-law's house at least once a week to spend time with her, and that hour or so each week was dearer to me than I'll ever be able to explain in a way that makes complete sense.

Unfortunately, Olivia suffered from colic, which is such a horrible condition that's quite common for many infants. It causes them to cry and cry and cry with no apparent causes or ways to calm down. I could sometimes get her to stop for a little bit by singing Taylor Swift songs or standing with her in my arms and distracting her with staring outside the window into the backyard or at the fan on the ceiling, but it pained me to see her turning so red and crying so much. I know I'm not a parent, so I don't know the complete pain it causes people with kids to see their own children hurt, but I know that it caused me enough pain to see my niece hurting to know that it must be absolutely unbearable.

When that guy I adored hurt me, I cried more than I usually do. You know who was always there for me? That sweet little baby girl. She listened to me, she let me cry, she cried with me, and she reminded me that there are a number of other people in my life who value me and who mean the world to me. Whether she knew it or not, she reminded me that, even when one guy makes me feel like I'm not good enough and not pretty enough and not worth enough of his time and energy, *I am still enough.* She made me feel loved when I felt completely unlovable.

I know that God brought her into this world in His exact time and with His exact purpose—Olivia is going to continue to change people's lives for the better, and I'm absolutely certain of that. I met her right when I needed someone to walk with me through my heartache, and she's continued to walk with me through that pain since the day she entered this world. Even when I lived thousands of miles away, I FaceTimed with her every week and spent as much time as possible with her when I was in town visiting my family.

Now Olivia has two adorable little sisters, Evie and Anna, and they've also been added blessings to everyone who meets them. Those little girls have the most beautiful and most contagious smiles you've ever seen in your entire life. I'm not biased—it's fact.

There's something about being an aunt that's more special than froyo, and I don't really know how to put it in the best words (even though words are supposed to be my thing). I honestly might not ever have kids (I've also been told that I can't), and that's fine, but being an aunt brings me enough joy to fill all of the oceans. I think part of the reason for that is because of the way Olivia originally changed my life in ways she doesn't yet understand.

For far too many years, I believed lies about who I was and what I wasn't—too talkative, not pretty enough, not smart enough, not dateable, unlovable, unaccepted, rejected, too broken, too much of a mess. While I definitely don't have it all together, I have much more confidence in who I am, and I don't focus as much on what I'm not. That's not important. What's important is that I continue to live and love boldly so that those around me can see Jesus and know that they are sufficient in Him.

Olivia helped to remind me of that, and she didn't even have to use any words to do so.

Maybe you're doing really well in life right now and are fortunate enough not to be going through any tough times or hardships. Or maybe you're in a rough patch full of more tears than all of your years combined and feel like you've been forgotten. Or maybe you're even somewhere in the middle and have a lot of great things going for you but also have been struggling at times.

Whatever season of life you're in right now, I hope that you know that *you are valued, you are loved, and you matter.* I hope that you have someone like Olivia come along and remind you of that, and I hope that you can be an Olivia to someone else, as well.

But I don't think that you have to be an aunt for something like that to happen. We often meet people who touch us and change us in incredible ways, and it's not necessarily always because of anything significant that they did—it's simply because they let us be who we are and reminded us that we are loved *just as we are.*

And you could also be that person to someone else.

My sister has also always been that person to me. Whenever I initially talk about her to other people, I make them aware of one truth: She's the most beautiful person I know, inside and out.

When I found out that the guy who had kissed me and then broken my heart was getting married, I wanted to get away for a little while. I looked at the website of my favorite author, Annie Downs, and saw that she was speaking at a conference in Tennessee. I had just finished reading *Let's All Be Brave*, a book that truly changed my heart in a million ways. I texted my sister to see if she would take a road trip to Tennessee with me. Her reply? "Absolutely!" She didn't even ask why or when or any details until later. That's just who she is—she's my ride or die, no questions asked.

I can vividly remember one time when we were young and home alone on somewhat of a dreary day. We heard a strange creepy noise coming from one of the closets in our house, but neither of us actually wanted to open the closet door. So we did what any logical girls would do: We grabbed golf clubs and went and sat on our front porch. This was the obvious solution for two reasons:

1. If you're ever in danger inside your home, it makes perfect sense to go wait on the front porch.
2. The best weapon of defense against anyone or anything making a noise in your closet is a golf club.

But, honestly, after a while, I wasn't even the least bit scared of what was possibly in the closet. I felt better knowing that my sister was right there with me, armed with a driver, ready to face anything right alongside me.

When my sister was born, I was elated to have little Steffie Robyn, as I called her, in my life. I even once pulled her arm out of its socket trying to get her out of her crib so that we could play together. Oopsies!

Since she came into my life more than 33 years ago, there have been too many adventures to count—and all of them have been worth every second. There's been laughter. There have been tears. There's been joy. There's been anger. There have been pleasant times. There have been fights. There's been patience. There's been frustration. There have been all of the things—but there's always been love, and there's always been trust.

I can't think of what life would have been like without her here with me, nor do I even want to imagine a world like that. She makes everywhere a better place to be. When you're sad, she'll scratch your back and make you laugh. When you need encouragement, she'll give you the best pep talk you've ever received. When you're angry, she'll soften you up so quickly and make you forget why you were even mad in the first place. When there's tension between people, she'll create peace. She sees the beauty in people that others often overlook, and she brings it to light. She reminds people that they are loved and that they matter.

I know that not everyone has siblings, and I know that not everyone who has siblings gets along with them. But I hope that you have your own Steffie Robyn—that person who is *always* there for you, no matter what, and will continue to be there for you, even when you're at your worst or going through the roughest of the rough patches. *Our hearts long for people like that.*

You never know what storms other people are facing. There are many different reasons people hurt—broken hearts, deaths of loved ones, lost jobs, financial hardships, broken friendships or family relationships, illnesses, uncomfortable or anxiety-causing situations at work or school—and we don't always know what's going on in each other's lives. That's just one more reason why it's so important to show each other love when the world around us continues to fill itself with lies and hate.

Because the more love we show to others to let them know that we care for them—their hurts, their celebrations, and simply their existences—the better this world will be.

SECTION 4

DON'T LET FEAR
HOLD YOU BACK

When You Take Chances on Yourself

I'm all about taking leaps of faith, even if those leaps mean that you literally have zero idea where you're going to land or how badly it might hurt if it doesn't turn out the way you thought.

Because I take those leaps with complete faith that God knows exactly what He's doing, even though I don't.

I taught high school for seven years before stepping away from it for four years and then returning to the classroom, and I truly love it now and loved it then. People don't always give teenagers enough credit for being incredible humans, but they are. Sure, some of them are not always nice and certainly have a ton of growing up to do, but I would argue that the majority of them actually have beautiful hearts that they're slowly learning how to share with the world.

In my sixth year of teaching, though, I knew that I only had one more year left in me (at least for a while, anyway). And, to be honest, the only reason I stayed for that final year was because there was one student I knew needed me there to finish her senior year, and I wasn't about to jump ship on her.

I loved those kids with all of my heart, but I had a stirring within me that I think God put there so that He could teach me some things about Him and about myself that I needed to learn. I enjoyed teaching them about life and walking through their journeys with them, but at the time, I was tired of putting numbers on paper and telling kids that they were only worth certain percentages. (I know that that's not the job of teachers and that grades don't actually tell kids what they're worth, but I wanted to step away from the grading and the numbers and the state standards and all of the other stuff and simply love and encourage people. I truly believe those four years away helped me become a better teacher who focuses even more on each student's heart.)

After a lot of prayer and tossing and turning, I decided that I was going to enter the corporate world and continue to pursue writing. In April of that seventh year of teaching, I let my supervisors know that I would not be signing my contract to return for the following year. No, I didn't have a plan. No, I had no idea what I was going to do for a career. But I wasn't worried about it.

I remember one of my friends giving me a pretty lengthy lecture about how I needed to get my act together and figure out how I was going to make a living. I had already figured it out, though—I was simply going to start applying for jobs and trust that the Lord would provide for me like He always had.

I had my friend Lucy come over one afternoon and show me how to use LinkedIn, and I began the process of looking for a job in an unfamiliar method and in an unfamiliar field. It was pretty daunting at first, but I had a weird confidence that I can't really describe well that led me to believe that everything was going to be alright—I had no reason to fret. Besides, the people around me were fretting enough for me and constantly asking me if I had found a job yet. I'd say that I hadn't, and the inevitable "Well, what are you going to do?" would follow.

What do you mean what am I going to do? I'm going to do the same thing I've been doing: keep applying for jobs and have faith that God will lead me to where He wants me to be.

And He did.

Somehow, by His glorious grace and a plan that I will never

in a million years understand, He led me to a financial services firm, where I took on the role of senior writer in the Marketing Department for more than two years. I knew basically nothing about financial services, but this company took a chance on me, and I'm forever grateful. I met some of my best friends and shared some of my favorite memories with them, whether it was at the bowling alley or while performing my own rendition of my soul sister Mariah's "All I Want for Christmas" to get everyone hyped up for the upcoming holiday party. (By the way, FINRA—a hugely important agency that essentially dictates all things financial-organization-related— was present for that performance, and I still didn't get fired, so my company was definitely a keeper in my book.)

I also learned about investing and retirement and stocks and bonds and Brexit and a ton of other financial industry stuff that I never thought I would know. I even took the Series 7 exam, which is by far the most difficult test I've ever taken. Maybe it's not as challenging for those who are more attuned with this area of business, but I wouldn't call it my strong suit by any means—none of it came naturally to me at all. I failed the test, but I learned a pretty sufficient amount along the way and gave myself a small pat on the back for at least attempting it.

I think that it's important to take chances on ourselves sometimes. The great Michael Scott (where are all of my lovers of *The Office*??) once looked David Wallace straight in the eyes and told him that David had no idea how high Michael could fly. And then Michael went on to create his own paper company that David eventually had to end up buying from Michael so that he wasn't such a threat to Dunder Mifflin. Michael knew that he was capable of more—so much more—and he acted upon the confidence he had in his abilities to do great things.

You, my friend, are capable of great things, too. I'm not telling you to quit your job, but I am encouraging you not to sit back and wish upon stars and candles and dandelions and 11:11 on the clock when you could be working toward making your dreams come true.

Sure, it wasn't my dream to become a writer at a financial services firm, but it was part of my story that needed to happen, as you'll later see.

If you don't take risks in life, how will you ever know what you're capable of doing?

And those opportunities you seize don't even have to be monumental or life-altering—they're often small moments that offer even only little bits of the self-assurance that you needed.

For me, I've often seen those moments come into play in my life when I have the chance to do something on my own that I've always wanted to do with my future guy. One time, it was merely stepping onto a Ferris wheel by myself when my heart was hurting more than it ever had.

For as far back as I can remember, I've wanted to ride a Ferris wheel with the man I love. I don't care if that sounds silly, and I don't have a logical reason why, other than it seems like something you would do with the person you love—you know, so that you can kiss and hold hands and talk about all of the things you want to talk about while you're stuck in a hopefully completely secured cable car/gondola thing. I feel like I've seen a lot of couples at fairs and carnivals hop on Ferris wheels together, and Marissa and Ryan had a special mutual affinity for them in *The O.C.*, so it's clearly the thing to do.

I actually don't even like carnivals or fairs much, but I love Ferris wheels. They're these gigantic slow-spinning circles of wonder, and they're slightly majestic for my previously mentioned reasons. However, I've never actually been anywhere remotely near a dreamboat man anytime I've ridden one, though the hope has always been there. Sometimes I'll even look around right before getting in line for a ticket to check to see if he's somehow miraculously heard a voice from the universe telling him to be at that exact place in that exact moment so that we could ride my dream Ferris wheel ride together.

That's yet to happen.

Shortly after moving to California, I went on the Ferris wheel at the Irvine Spectrum Center, a local shopping area with some fun activities included in addition to all of the retail stores. This came at a time in my life when I was truly struggling to get over that broken heart that felt like it ripped a huge chunk of my world apart and when I was still hoping with all of the hope in my aching heart that somehow things would magically work out with that guy.

It's a lonely place to be when you're sitting at the top of the Ferris wheel all by yourself, your heart longing for that one person you want sitting next to you forever.

But in that very same moment, I realized something: I'm perfectly fine sitting alone in a Ferris wheel gondola. Sure, I'd love someone by my side, but it's not a requirement to my happiness. Growing up on Disney and romantic comedies made me believe at an early age that I was meant to grow up, fall in love, get married, and live a content life. What reality has taught me, though, is that such an ideal timeline of events is not for everyone. (And, yes, I do know that even those who are married don't have perfect lives and have their fair shares of troubles and rough patches in their relationships.)

Life is going to throw junk your way that you don't even want to attempt to hit, but that stuff can't break you. It's in those times when you can learn a great amount about yourself and what you're actually capable of handling and capable of achieving.

Moving to California all by myself during such a painful time in my life might not have been the best idea in many people's eyes, but it was exactly what I needed—and God knew that. He called me out there for His purpose and on purpose, and I had no choice but to follow His calling, even if that meant packing up my broken pieces and bringing them along, as well.

You can't truly heal unless you're willing to see that you're broken and in need of mending.

Don't let fear hold you back from healing. Don't let fear hold you back from taking chances that might lead to incredible opportunities that you never thought possible and probably never saw coming. Don't let fear hold you back from *truly living*.

It's not easy to step outside of your comfort zone, but I've heard it said that nothing great happens inside that zone, and I believe that it's a pretty accurate statement. If you're not willing to step out into the unknown once in a while, then those surprise bits of glory that you didn't see coming won't ever happen.

My sweet friend, please take that step. Please seize your moments. Send that text. Make that move. Pursue that dream. Start that conversation. Buy that ticket. Sign up for that class. Apply for that job. Do whatever it is you need to do to make sure that you are living fully and living boldly without worrying about all of the bad things that can happen. No, it won't always end perfectly, but at least you will have believed in yourself enough to fight for yourself.

And sometimes fighting for yourself is the bravest thing you can do.

~ ~

When you take chances on yourself and fight for yourself, it often winds up meaning that you're taking a chance on love, as well.

There are supposedly five love languages (as you might recall, I'm a quality time girl all the way), but there's one that's missing from the list: sports. Sports are, hands down, my true love language.

On more than one occasion, I've sat in the exact same spot for nearly 12 straight hours (minus some bathroom breaks here and there) watching college football. I've painted my entire body blue (also on more than one occasion) to show my fandom and win a spirit contest at Dallas Mavericks games. And now that I can watch basically any sport on my phone in any location, my life has changed significantly.

There are so many exciting moments in all sports, especially in college football. I'll never forget watching a West Virginia-Texas game while I was living in California in the fall of 2018. West

Virginia was down 41-34 with the clock ticking down at the end of the fourth quarter. The Mountaineers scored and then had a choice—kick the extra point to send the game into overtime or go for the two-point conversion and win the whole thing right then and there. The commentators mentioned that the West Virginia coach had a history of being a bit of a risk taker in those types of situations and thought he'd go for it. Sure enough, they were right—Coach Holgorsen called for the two-point play.

A man after my own heart.

Those West Virginia players walked away with that 42-41 win because they had trusted their coach and his plan. He knew their abilities, and he knew that he had prepared them for that moment. I love seeing stories like that as they're happening (unless it's against my team, of course). They're reminders that life is full of opportunities that we can either seize or let pass us by far too quickly.

I honestly have more moments of kicking the extra point instead of going for the two points than I'd like to admit. I can think back to exact instances when I wish I would have said something that I didn't or do something differently than I did. It serves me absolutely no value to dwell on those missed chances, but they do motivate me to take more risks in my present.

I think one of the greatest risks of all is loving people. Whether it's giving your heart away to the one who makes it beat out of control or giving your heart to show others that they matter and that you care, there are significant risks involved. There's the risk of that love being unrequited. There's the risk of that love being questioned and frowned upon by society. There's the risk of that love being given to individuals who have been labeled as undeserving.

Here's the thing, though: No matter what the risks are, everyone needs love.

One day not too long after that game, I was at the beach watching the waves come in when I noticed a man and woman and their precious daughter. The little girl was playing in the water with her dad and begging her mom to come join them. I watched as the mom barely let the water touch her toes before telling the sweet pig-tailed cutie that it was freezing. (The Pacific Ocean is very cold, especially during the "winter" months. For some reason, though, kids never seem to notice things like temperatures.)

But then the little girl said "Please, will you, Mom? It will be so fun!" The woman had a sudden change of heart, went for the two-point conversion, and dashed out into the icicles—because she knew that the risk of freezing was nothing compared to the memories she was making with her daughter and husband and the joy they were all experiencing together. She chose love, and it was worth it.

Sure, not every risk you take will end the way you want it to. Sometimes you'll go for that two-point conversion and walk away empty-handed. But sometimes you won't. Like those West Virginia Mountaineers, maybe you simply need to trust the ultimate Coach and His plan. And maybe that means you choose love with the complete confidence that it's worth it.

My sweet friend, don't settle for the extra point when you know that you're capable of getting two.

20

Because It's OK to Trust
Your Own Advice

I need to stop asking people for advice.

Like, seriously.

I have this really bad habit of asking way too many people's opinions when I'm trying to make a big decision. Of course, by big decision, I mean what I'm going to say in a text message to a guy I like. I know. I'm 13.

There was a guy I thought I might have feelings for not too long ago, and I wanted to send him a text. I typed it up and sent it to one friend and then copied and pasted it and sent it to two other friends to get their stamps of approval. You know what, though? No matter what they thought or said, it was my words that I put together and what I wanted to say. What did it matter what they thought?

Sure, it's good to get advice and wise counsel from others at times, but I feel like I should be able to handle a simple text message on my own. The words need to be crafted by me because the guy needs to fall for me, not for my friends. He needs to hear my voice, not theirs.

Whenever I do this, I usually spend about seven to nine seconds or so questioning why I'm asking so many people what they think, and then I remember all too well: *I want validation.* I want them to support my feelings and actions, and I want them to tell me that they would do the same thing that I would do (or that I already did). But that's not always the case, and a feeling that I absolutely detest replaces that nonexistent validation that I needed: insecurity. In this particular instance, I had suddenly become entirely too anxious that I'd done something stupid, and that guy would think I was stupid and would want to make fun of me the same way the boy in high school wanted to make fun of me.

And then I have to talk myself off of the ledge—*Natalie, let that go. You're so far past that. You are a strong and confident woman, and you don't need validation from your friends or from him or from anyone. If you want to text someone, don't hesitate—send the text. You do you, girl.*

I wasn't always able to give myself these little pep talks, and I'll admit that even some of them nowadays aren't necessarily as effective as I would like for them to be. But I do fully know in my heart that I am who I am, and my identity is not determined by what a guy thinks of a text. My worth is not determined by anyone's opinion of me. My value is not determined by how ridiculously inexperienced and quirky I am.

I am valued, I am loved, and I matter. And nothing—not one single imperfect text or one single thing or one single person on this entire planet or any other planet—can ever change that or take that truth away from me.

To be honest, it's challenging sometimes to be reminded by others or by myself that I'm in my 30s and haven't been in an actual relationship, and I occasionally find myself feeling more than slightly pathetic to be my age and still this single. I go through seasons of being OK with it and seasons of feeling lonely. I would say that my current state is one in which I've transitioned out of that lonely one into one that's more comfortable, but I know that there are times when the enemy brings those destructive thoughts and lies into my mind.

But it's in those times that I need to channel that strong and confident woman I am and let her be the one to take over those negative self-perceptions—*I can't let people's words and opinions of me change what I think or say about myself.* And I hope that you won't let other people's words and opinions of you change what you think or say about yourself. They cannot define who you are— unless you let them.

And we don't need to try to influence other people's views of themselves with our unwarranted thoughts, either. We don't know what everyone else is struggling with or what storms they might be facing in their lives. Instead of judging others or assuming you know them, perhaps give them a little grace, or even take the time to get to know them. You might find that your attitude toward a person can change when you actually take time to learn more about him or her with a heart perspective.

We're not all going to live our lives the same way, and that's a good thing. People don't have to express joy the same way you do. People don't have to have the same relationship timelines that you do or send the same text messages that you would. People don't have to spend the same amount of time at their jobs or in their hobbies as you do. People don't have to like all of the same movies or foods or pastimes or whatever as you.

And you don't have to be like everyone else, either. It's important to be genuine, to be real. People can't know the real you and your heart if you aren't being who you actually are. If they judge you for being you, then so be it. Your identity shouldn't be the result of what someone else thinks it should be. That goes for all types of relationships—with strangers who know nothing about you, with family members who know everything about you, with your friends who are your ride-or-die lifers, with acquaintances, with people you might look at as enemies, and with the person whom you love or are dating.

Be authentically you, my friend—it's harder for people to know your heart if you don't truly know it yourself.

I love my friend Cristy. She was my sister's Sunday school teacher when I was in ninth grade, and I then became her go-to babysitter for years. Her oldest daughter is now in college (WHERE DOES THE ACTUAL TIME GO?!), so Cristy and I have been through many seasons together. She has walked with me through them all, and she is always one of the first people I call or text when I need solid advice.

The wisdom I receive from Cristy is a lot different from the other opinions I often seek. I don't ask her what type of text message I should send someone or whether or not I should text him at all. I go to her for the real stuff—the deep, often life-altering stuff. She has prayed with me through all of the hurt, all of the joys, all of the adventures, all of the faith moments, and so much more. She's a rock for me, and I cherish her insight. She is probably the most genuine person I've ever met in my entire life, and there's never been a moment after spending time with her that I haven't left feeling better. Feeling loved. Feeling encouraged. Feeling brave.

The difference is that, when I go to Cristy, I'm not going for validation or because I have anxiety. I go to Cristy because I trust her completely with my heart, and I know that she's only going to speak truth into it. That's not to say that I don't trust my other friends and that they don't have valid and helpful things to say, but there's something about Cristy that lights a fire in my soul. She's an absolute Godsend into my life, and I would trust her with anything and everything. Her opinions, to me, aren't merely opinions— they're little treasures of wisdom and hope and joy and honesty and transparency and love and deep caring and all of the goodness from the Lord ever to add to my heart and carry around with me.

I encourage you to find your own Cristy—someone who speaks life into you and reminds you that people's opinions of you don't actually matter. Someone who reminds you that you are loved just as you are. Someone who reminds you that prayer is powerful. Someone who reminds you that God is for you and not against you. Someone who reminds you that you are a treasure. Someone who reminds you to be bold. Someone who reminds you that people deserve grace and love from you. Someone who reminds you that you're worth people's time.

Someone who reminds you that you need to remind yourself of all of these things more often.

~ ~

So, yes, there are absolutely times when it's good to get advice from the people in your life, especially when it comes to those big decisions for which you want people to pray with you and walk alongside you as you seek the right path you should take. But then there are times when you need to shut out advice and opinions and not even ask for them and simply let your heart lead the way. You're a big girl now, and you're perfectly capable of making decisions on your own—you know, like my decision to text the guy.

If you fail, you fail. But at least you tried and were brave enough to step out and attempt something on your own. I've mentioned plenty of times that I'm not perfect, and I continue to prove that over and over. I had my RAV4 for almost nine years before I realized I didn't know as much about that car—or how to operate a car, apparently—as I thought I did. I mean, I used to have a bus license, and I had been driving by myself for almost 18 years at that point, so I was pretty sure I had it all down.

Sadly, I was mistaken.

It turns out that, for almost nine years, I wasn't using the correct lights at night. I thought that if you clicked the lights two turns forward, you were using the brights. So I always just clicked the turner once forward. Sometimes my friends would make comments like "Are you sure your lights are on?" when they were with me in the car, but I assured them that the lights just looked dim but were actually on.

I was in a rental car on a visit to Texas after I had moved to California and was trying to figure out how to turn on the lights, so I pulled the manual out of the glove compartment, and it said something about turning the thing twice for normal lights and then pushing the lights lever forward to turn on the brights. When I turned on those lights, some lights that had been off in my brain for almost nine years finally turned on, and I had an epiphany: *Wait a second. What if my car works the same way?*

You probably already knew the answer to that one.

Sure enough, I tested it out the next time I was in my car, and then I checked my car's own manual. Yep, I'd been driving at night without my actual lights FOR ALMOST NINE YEARS. To answer the question you might be wondering, I have no idea how I was never pulled over for this.

But I felt like such a fool.

And I'm pretty sure that won't be the last time I do something that I consider to be foolish. Be it send a lame text or say the wrong thing or whatever, I'm going to mess up. That's where grace comes into the picture. I love people, and I feel like I've gotten a lot better over the years about giving people grace and loving them in spite of their faults and mistakes, but it's more of a struggle for me to show that same grace and love to myself. I don't really care if other people think I'm flawed or weird or bad at something, but I have a lot of trouble when I feel like I've messed up big time and disappointed myself.

To be honest, I think that's one of the big reasons why I've struggled so much in the past with feeling rejected by guys. I constantly wondered if there was something wrong with me that made me not appealing to them, and over time, that became more of a *me* thing than a *them* thing—if all of them weren't interested, then that must mean there was something about me that was off or not enough (which—again, let me engrain this into your brain and your heart—is a lie I hope none of you lets enter your head).

And that made me feel like a complete disappointment to myself.

What I've learned, though, is that my flaws are part of who I am. And your flaws are part of who you are. Sure, there are some real flaws that definitely need to be addressed and overcome, but many of the "flaws" we see in ourselves aren't actually flaws to anyone but ourselves. I'm not a car expert, and I'm not the girl who turns all of the heads and gets all of the guys.

But I'm me, and that's good enough for me.

So don't worry so much about whether or not you're doing everything right in life. You won't always, and that's OK. You'll learn some valuable lessons by messing up. Just don't be afraid to listen to your heart and not rely on everyone else's advice and opinions regarding how you should live and the actions that you should or shouldn't take or the things that you should or shouldn't say.

Send that text, girl. You'll eventually be glad you did.

21

When Dating Apps Aren't Your Thing

I watched a lot of *The Mindy Project* a few years ago, and I started to get a bit nervous that maybe I wasn't doing something right in life. I know it's just a TV show, but I feel like it portrayed a great deal of accuracy in terms of people's dating lifestyles.

The thing that got me a little apprehensive is how easily Mindy is able to get dates in the show with practically any guy she meets and how many guys she attracts. I don't feel like I ever walk into a bar or restaurant or store or office and immediately attract anyone. Mindy does, and it doesn't even seem like she has to try very hard at all.

Am I doing something wrong over here?

At the time, all of my single friends (well, there were two of them left) had been going on a lot of dates, as well. Granted, they had been using some of the dating apps, but even when I briefly tried those, I didn't have nearly as much luck as they did. I know that comparison is the thief of joy and blah, blah, blah, but it's a little bit difficult not to be fully aware that pretty much every single human around me is either married, in a serious relationship, active on the dating scene, or a toddler.

And then there's me.

I know I'm picky and have pretty high standards, but I don't think that's a bad thing. I don't want to end up with someone just to end up with someone—I want to end up with the *right* someone. But I used to have the mindset that there's something about me that repels guys. Why else would I have TWO different guys cancel on being my wedding dates? Why else would I have a guy tell me that I'm one of his favorite people, but then he wouldn't ever actually date me? Why else would a guy lead me on for months and then leave and break my heart? Why else would a guy kiss me and make me pie-crust promises and then pursue another woman?

It was because of my guy repellant, obviously.

While I'm somewhat joking about the repellant thing, it's really easy to get caught up in a mindset like that when it seems like the world around you is moving on and growing up without you. I know I'm not the only single girl still in existence, and I know I won't be the last single girl ever to walk the earth, but that doesn't mean it doesn't feel that way sometimes. I don't think I'm alone in these feelings, either. I know there are others out there like me who are hoping and waiting and praying and wishing really hard for those special fellas to come swoop into our lives and make a love story feel like a real thing that isn't only something conjured up in our hearts' imaginations.

Whatever you do, don't give up that hope.

You may not be married or in love by the time you wanted to or by the time all of your friends and family members are, but that doesn't mean that it will never happen for you. Maybe you truly feel in your heart that you're 100-percent ready for it to happen—but maybe he's not. Maybe your lobster needs his heart to ripen just a little bit more until he's ready to meet you. Or maybe you think you're ready, but something else needs to happen in your life first before you let someone else in it permanently. Whatever the reason, you still have every right to hope that you'll still get your own version of a romcom ending.

And I'll be cheering for you every step of the way to help you keep that hope alive. I tried a lot of different methods (well, in my opinion) to get over the most broken broken heart I ever had. And, yes, that includes dating apps.

Oh, the dating apps.

I know that online dating and all of the different apps are often the best way to meet people nowadays, but I am still struggling to get completely on board with them. I fully support my friends who use them, and I even go back and forth with them (I've created and deleted accounts more times that I can count). I understand that they work for some people—I know people who have married the individuals they've met on Bumble and Tinder and Coffee Meets Bagel and a number of the other digital Cupids.

But, just like coordinated dancing, they aren't for everyone.

I started with Bumble. I immediately felt really strange and rather mean swiping through all of the pictures of guys I had never met and essentially judging them (and I don't like to be a judger) based on their profile pictures and brief (if any) descriptions of themselves. And I'll admit that one of my biggest problems was that I was comparing each and every one of them to the guy who truly had a hold on my heart that wouldn't let go. I honestly only wanted to end up with him, and I knew that no other guy who happened to swipe the same way as I did was ever going to measure up to him. Tunnel vision is real, sister.

But I still gave it the old college try.

I even had some conversations with some of them, but here's the thing you probably already know about Bumble: The girl has to make the first move. Sure, I wouldn't exactly call myself shy, but I'm also not very experienced at the whole dating thing and what people say to people they're interested in. I'm trying not to be ashamed to say that most of my opening liners were, "Hey, [insert name here]! How's it going?"

I know—I cringe reading it to myself now, too.

Sometimes I tried to come up with something witty to say based on the guys' profiles, but many of them didn't give me much material to work with at all. And then most of the conversations died out pretty quickly. When I initially tried dating apps for the first time, I met one of the guys in person, and I knew within the first 12 seconds of meeting him that there was zilch between us. We ate some food and chatted for a while, and then I told him that it was time for me to get going. Something along the lines of the following conversation ensued.

Guy: *You don't want to go somewhere else?*
Me: *No, I don't. I'm calling for my Uber now.*
Guy: *You can share an Uber with me, and I can take care of it.*
Me: (definitely not wanting to be in a car with that man and for him to know where I lived) *That's not necessary. Plus, it doesn't make sense because it's out of your way.*
Guy (as I was getting into my Uber): *It was really nice to meet you.*
Me: *Ditto. And at least now we know that we weren't meant for each other. Good luck to you.*

Maybe you think it's rude to be blunt, but I think it's better to be honest with someone than to lead him on. Plus, if he didn't realize by that point that there was zero chemistry between us and that I was not interested in him, then it became essential to make it crystal clear.

Then there was the guy I never met because, after a few days of messaging on the app, he mentioned wanting to meet me. Then he told me I have a nice body. I told him that I'm a runner, and he said it shows. He should have stopped there, but he let some of his male instincts take over, and he asked me if I have a nice butt. He said he's really into butts.

To quote Ariana Grande, "thank u, next."

Oy vey. I thought that it would be a good idea to try the app option again later after I had moved to California. I'm not sure if I thought my experience would be more positive or if I simply needed to branch out and try to meet people in a place that was so new to me, but I recreated an account. I still wasn't a fan, but I was in a weird season in which I felt like I needed to be in a relationship. In my heart, I felt like I wasn't going to find what I was looking for on a dating app—or in any guy, for that matter—yet I stuck with it. One guy I had chatted with found out that I don't drink, and he told me "hard pass" and stopped talking to me. Many of my conversations went nowhere, and I was actually fine with that.

I met one of the guys for froyo, and as I expected (I clearly had the right mindset, huh?), I knew within about three seconds this time that he wasn't my person. I think we both knew it, and he didn't seem too interested in me, either. When I left, I wished him well, and I never saw him or heard from him again.

The way people meet and fall in love has changed in so many ways, compared to how it used to happen years ago, but that's just part of the society in which we live now. Around that same time of the failed attempt with dating apps again, one of my friends had mentioned someone she had heard of on Instagram, which resulted in me meeting with a matchmaker. Think of the movie *Hitch*, and it's a similar concept. It actually sounded pretty interesting and maybe even effective, but then she told me what the costs were for either a three-month contract or a six-month contract, and I had the same reaction that Elle Woods had when Vivian Kensington introduced herself as Warner's fiancée.

I'm sorry. I just hallucinated. What?

Needless to say, I won't be part of the next Albert Brennaman/ Allegra Cole success story. I'm still trying to have high hopes for my dream of meeting someone unexpectedly and out of the blue, like me being hit in the face with a football or frisbee at a park or beach, and the guy runs over to check to make sure that I'm OK, and sparks fly.

A girl can dream.

Dating apps and matchmakers don't have to be part of your story. They work for some people, and I'm genuinely happy for those people. But they aren't for all of us.

I don't know how I'll meet someone, but I do know that I don't want to be so caught up in trying to find him that I get completely lost. There's so much life to live, and there's so much love to give others. I want my focus to remain on being thankful for those things and those people already in my life and pursue them.

After all, life isn't one big game of capture the flag—there are too many people in this world who need love and need to know that they are valued. Do I want to fall in love with my person and be loved unconditionally by him? Absolutely. But I can't stop my life entirely to go searching for that one flag that might not be ready for me to find yet.

And I've learned that tunnel vision isn't always the best thing to have.

For so long, I was so focused on this one guy—the guy who clearly didn't want me enough to hang around or make me feel like I was even the slightest bit valued by him—that I ignored a couple of really great guys who potentially could have become more than friends to me. I had a conversation with one of them later and asked why we had drifted, and he said something to me that pierced my heart—mainly because he was completely right.

"You seemed like you had a lot going on and not necessarily room for anybody else at that time."

Bless my heart. I felt awful. I apologized to him, and he was incredibly sweet about it and assured me that he completely understood—both back then and when we had the conversation—but it didn't change the fact that I never want to make anyone feel like there isn't any more room for people in my life. My job is to love people and love them unconditionally, not make them feel like I don't have the capacity to do so.

I can't ever go back and change the past, and I've accepted the things I've done and haven't done. Besides, if things had gone differently in any manner, I might not have ended up in California for the time that I was there. I needed that time to heal and to be reminded of God's sufficiency and constant love for me. I needed to be out there on my own to realize that I'm never actually on my own. And I needed to be out there to be trained and equipped for what God wanted me to do when He brought me back to Dallas.

But I hope that I will never again let anyone feel like there isn't room in my life for him or her to be a part of it.

I fully trust that God has kept me single for 35 years for a reason—His reason—and I know that He will provide love for me in big ways, whether that means I find my lobster or continue to rock this whole life thing as a single gal with no plus-one in sight. Either way, I know that He's still going to fill my heart with more love than I could ever imagine, and He's going to surround me with a community of people who will love me as I am. He's done it before, and I know that He'll do it again.

And I will continue to believe every word of the song "Do It Again" each time I sing it.

I don't know what you're going through in life. Maybe you're like me and wish that you could find love in a world that seems to be more challenging for the single folks every day. I hope that you don't lose hope. I hope that you keep pressing on through the storms of heartache that try to knock you down. I hope that you know that you are worthy and enough with or without someone else standing by your side.

If dating apps are for you, then by all means, use them. I hope that you meet your lobster on one of them and work on your own love story together. If they're not for you, though, there's nothing wrong with you—at all. And, despite what our society might often make you think, dating apps are not the only way to meet people nowadays. It can still happen through friends, on a plane, at church, in the grocery store produce section, in the Target parking lot, in your workplace, or at a million other places that aren't popping into my head right now.

Just please always remember that your relationship status does not define your worth, and it does not define who you are as a person. You are valued, you are loved, and you matter just the way you are, and that's never going to change.

So don't fret if people aren't swiping right to capture your heart—there's a much greater love already surrounding you that isn't concerned with your pictures and profile description.

My dear sister, you are loved by the One who will love you more than anyone else in the entire world ever could.

22

Because Sometimes Stepping Out of Your Comfort Zone Means Moving to California

In the fall of 2016, I was fresh into that broken heart that I've talked about a ton already and going through a pretty rough time in my life. I had never felt that strongly for someone, and I guess I hadn't expected things to end the way they had—with me picking up the pieces of my shattered heart and hopes after someone I thought actually cared for me showed me how wrong I was.

On top of that, I began having those kidney issues that eventually required the three surgeries in 2017. The physical pain was masked quite a bit by my emotional pain, but it was still there. I felt like I wasn't myself for a really long time. I'm normally a positive and energetic person, but there was a dimmed spark in me that I didn't try very hard to hide.

When people asked me how I was doing, my only answer was always "I'm OK," and in my head, I would echo that with a line from my favorite Taylor Swift song ("All Too Well"—go listen to it ASAP, please) by saying that I might have been OK, but I wasn't fine at all. That was the second time period when I played that song on repeat every day on the way to work in the morning after listening to a segment of "The Musers" on The Ticket. A lot of days kind of felt like I was just floating, but I also felt like I was sinking from the heaviness that I felt I was carrying.

I remember going to a massage place with my sister for my birthday that year, and when mine was finished, the massage therapist and I had the following conversation.

MT: *I don't mean to pry, but have you recently gone through or are you currently going through a heartache?*
Me: *How did you know that? Did my sister talk to you?*
MT: *No, no. You're really tight right here (pointing to the area between his armpits and chest), and that's often an indication of emotional pain. It's as if the pain you feel from the heart physically causes everything to be drawn toward the heart, developing an extreme tightness. I've never worked on anyone as tight as you in that area.*
Me: *Oh, good. That's special.*

Wow. The massage therapist hitting me with some straight-up truth. I know that I shouldn't have been sarcastic with him, but I was not in a mood to be reminded that I was hurting—or to know that it was so apparent to someone who knew literally zilch about me other than me telling him that I was a runner and have tight hips.

I spent a significant amount of time in prayer during that season, but those prayers mainly consisted of me asking God why I had to go through what I was feeling and dealing with and begging that He would take my feelings and the pain away. As much as I wanted to rely solely on God in my darkest moments, I didn't always do a great job of that. I relied way too much on my people helping me through it and talking about it when I was up for talking about it. And I relied a lot on running to help me escape from the world and simply do something mindless that gave me peace.

Unfortunately, though, running can't sustain me forever. That became painfully obvious when my kidney issues became too much, and I suffered through that annual 8-mile race that Thanksgiving and then didn't even make it to the start line of the half marathon I had been training for that took place a few weeks later.

That same week that the race didn't happen, my company held its yearly holiday party, and I walked away with what I didn't know at the time would be such a life-changing gift. Each year, there was a huge raffle at this party—I'm talking insanely awesome prizes, such as expensive appliances and electronics, gift cards, and even plane tickets. It's very rare that I win anything big, so I wasn't expecting much. I would have been thrilled with a gift card. I had a weird feeling going into that evening, though—a strange stirring in my heart that I can't perfectly describe. Then it happened: The raffle host called my name when he drew for the two plane tickets to anywhere in the continental U.S. As I walked to claim them, I knew that there was only one place I wanted to go if Hawaii wasn't an option: Newport Beach. And there was only one person I wanted to go with me.

The more I thought about it, though, the more I thought it might be better to give the tickets to my sister and her husband rather than inviting her on a fun escape from reality with me. Sure, I really wanted to take a sisters trip with her, but they had just gotten married and weren't able to go on a honeymoon together. I called her on my way home to tell her that I had won tickets for them, but then she was the one who said that we should take a girls trip together, instead.

That next June, we were on our way to a place I had only imagined. I had read all of Robin Jones Gunn's *Christy Miller Series* books and fallen in love with Newport Beach—you know, a place I had never actually experienced. (By the way, I highly recommend this series for all young women. And old women. And any women currently breathing.) *The O.C.* apparently wasn't even actually filmed in Newport Beach or anywhere in Orange County (don't get me started on that lie that I believed for so long), so I had zero clue what it was like. I only had all of my mental images that I had allowed

Christy and Todd to paint in my head as they grew up together and fell in love with one another there.

It was a remarkable trip that I'll hold in my heart forever, and I kept thinking the entire time about how beautiful of a place Orange County is. It was incredibly peaceful, even with all of the summer crowds. I remember a moment when my sister and I were walking on the beach together, and she said something about liking taking a vacation there, but she could never live that lifestyle every single day of her life. *I could.* I brushed that thought out of my head because it seemed silly at the time.

On the plane ride home, I was reading a completely different book by Robin Jones Gunn about one of the spinoff characters who is friends with Christy, and the young woman in the book is trying to figure out the next chapter in her life. She prays about it and feels God calling her to Santa Barbara. I won't give away everything in the book, but let's just say it really works out great for her because of the guy she meets and falls for while she's on vacation. I set the book down and began to pray, too.

God, I know that this is just a book, and this character isn't even real, but why did she know exactly what to do, and I'm still trying to figure everything out? Why can't you give me clear answers, too? I don't feel content in what I'm doing in life, and I'm hurting—a lot. What am I supposed to do, God?

And then I heard a quiet but powerful voice that I couldn't ignore: *Move to California.*

That wasn't the answer I wanted or expected.

No. I just read that in the book, and I had a great vacation there. I'm very thankful to You for that, but I'm not moving there. New plan, please.

But you can't just brush aside something that God is calling you to do, and I eventually had to listen. I started applying for jobs, which was a pretty discouraging feat most of the time. Apparently a lot of companies aren't interested in hiring some girl from a completely different state when they can easily hire others who are more local and can actually show up to interviews at the drop of a hat and not have to make arrangements at work and book travel and possibly be compensated for relocation and whatnot. I can't tell you how many hours I spent filling out seemingly endless applications for companies from which I would either never hear or from which I'd receive one-line emails saying they were pursuing other candidates.

Rejection hurts.

In the meantime, I was dealing with the kidney issues and had two unexpected surgeries in August. When I woke up from the second one, I had a voicemail offering me a job at one of the places I had applied in Orange County. I was still pretty loopy from the anesthesia, but I remember turning to my mom and sister in the hospital and saying "I got the job!" I know that they wanted to be excited for me, but the looks on their faces showed that they were more shocked than anything.

Join the club, ladies.

After that moment, everything began happening so quickly, and I didn't have a lot of time left in Dallas—only about three weeks, to be sort of exact. I'd be lying if I told you that I wasn't a little scared. I wasn't afraid of not knowing anyone in a new location—meeting new people and making friends is a pastime that I cherish—but I was a little afraid of leaving my people. I knew that I wouldn't see my parents every Sunday and get a big hug from my mom right before I left their house. I wouldn't be able to get together with my sister as often or stop by her place and see her and her husband and their crazy dogs and cat, and that tore me up inside. I wouldn't be able to hang out with my niece (this was before precious Evie and Anna were born) every weekend and visit with my brother and sister-in-law. I never knew that I could love a tiny human who wasn't even my own child this much until I became an aunt. And I won't get started on the feelings I had thinking about all of my friends and my favorite froyo place—we'd be here for hours.

But, even though I knew that it was likely going to be one of the most difficult things I'd ever done, I knew that it was right, and

I let myself get incredibly excited. (Plus, I actually didn't have much time to get too sad about it because my life became an actual tornado for the next few weeks.) And I knew that the people who are in my tribe forever are the ones I will never lose, regardless of where I am or where they are. I truly believe with all of my heart that love is much stronger than distance.

And no amount of miles will ever change that.

My last three weeks in Dallas were kind of a blur, and it was probably good that it happened the way it did (I mean, of course it was). I didn't really have time to feel much more than the slight twinges of fear I mentioned. There honestly wasn't even time to feel reminiscent or emotional—there was way too much anxiety going on to make sure that I got my apartment packed up and car loaded. I only took what would fit in my car, so everything else had to go.

I knew the trip was going to take a little less than 21 hours to complete, but I didn't want to break up the drive evenly—it seemed a lot more daunting—so I decided driving a little more than 15 hours on the first day and then a little more than five on the second would be better (which is weird because I hate numbers in increments of five). I don't think I'd ever been in a car for 15 hours at a time, but it seemed doable.

Please take note: Spending 15+ hours in a car is A VERY LONG TIME, so please make sure that fully sinks in before you start the trip. However, it is indeed possible, though sometimes painful. Wintergreen Tic Tacs helped us survive.

Thankfully, my sister made the trek with me. I honestly don't know how I would have endured that journey without her without going completely insane. Sure, she slept some in the passenger seat (she was awake most of the time), but she also drove for a couple of hours to give me some rest, which was very helpful—after all, how else was I going to catch up on my Instagram feed?

You know, the important things.

It took a fairly long time to get out of Texas (it's beyond huge), and we only got pulled over once (THANK YOU, state trooper, for letting us drive away with only a warning). After we parted from Texas, even though we drove through lots of desert stretches, it was an incredibly scenic drive. Plus, we had some really solid playlists to keep us going—special thanks to Taylor Swift (obvi), Kelsea Ballerini, Thomas Rhett, Matt Wertz, and all of those old-school 90s pop artists on Spotify. I feel bad for all of the people who have to make long drives without my sister along for the ride—they're missing out. (As a side note, she's not available to be a passenger upon request, so please do not inquire.)

It was a whirlwind of an adventure getting out there and getting me moved in. I'll forever be thankful that she made that trip with me, and it wasn't until I dropped her off at the airport that Sunday morning that it hit me like a linebacker sacking an unsuspecting quarterback who was looking downfield: *I'm all alone in California, and I don't know a soul.*

The first three months there were rather tough, and I cried more than I want to admit. When I started to feel all of the feelings when I was at work, I would go lock myself in the bathroom, slide down the wall, sit on the floor (I know—gross), put my face in my hands, and then just let all of the tears fall. And then I would try to wait long enough for most of the splotchy redness on my face to disappear before I returned to my desk.

I knew that I wanted and needed friendships, so as soon as I moved out there, I started asking people to go grab coffee. I actually hate coffee, but it seemed like a good way to chat with people and get to know them better. I got plugged in at my church pretty quickly and frequently invited myself places with people. I have no shame, my friends. I also joined a flag football league, which was a ton of fun and reminded me what it was like to be part of team sports again.

Even after getting to know people and becoming more familiar with the area, though, I still didn't feel settled. Sure, I loved being able to go to the beach whenever I wanted or go hiking in the breathtaking hills that overlooked the ocean, but there was still something missing. I remember breaking down into a reservoir of tears one Saturday afternoon while I was driving (I probably should have pulled over because my eyes were filled with way too much water to see clearly) and crying out to God: *"Why am I out here? I listened to You and came to California, but why does it still hurt so much? What am I supposed to do here?"*

And then that same quiet but powerful voice that I've become so familiar with whispered back: *Don't you trust me?*

Yes. Yes, I do. And I guess I need to live more like I do.

I'm not going to say that everything became incredibly easy after that moment, but there was a peace in my heart that hadn't been there before. For the first time since I had moved to California, I truly felt God working in my heart and doing something big. I knew that He had called me there with purpose, and I became more excited for whatever He had in store for me.

23

When You Dare to Hope, Pursue Adventures, and Make Mistakes

I love the honesty and genuineness that kids bring to pretty much any situation—even when their truthfulness stings.

One Sunday when I was living in California, my friend Monique asked if I could help out in the children's ministry at church, which I definitely didn't mind. I led a group of high school girls and spoke often for the junior high kids, so I figured I might as well work with the younger ones at some point, too. I love kids, so I knew it would be fun.

And apparently truth-telling, as well.

I was making bracelets with two sweet girls whom we'll call Avery and Sydney and asking them questions about their lives. They liked saying how old they were at the time, so more than once, Sydney told me that she was 7, and Avery reminded me that she was 8. When Sydney asked me how old I was, I told her, and she replied with something that stung a little, mainly because I wasn't expecting it.

"You're older than my parents."

Oy. When I used to babysit and teach swim lessons and work at a daycare center, the parents were always older than I was. It was weird to realize in that moment that I was working with kids who easily could have been my kids or whose parents could have been my younger siblings—or were even young enough that they could have been my former students. (It's crazy to think that some of my former students are in their late 20s or have already hit the big 3-0.) I always knew that aging is a thing, but I don't know that I was expecting it to happen to me—at least not this quickly.

Avery then told me her parents' ages—34 and 35, so at least I wasn't completely ancient yet—and asked me if I had kids. I said no and that I wasn't married, which was followed by what those precious little unfiltered mouths always seem to ask.

Avery: Why aren't you married?
Me: Just hasn't happened yet.
Avery: You should find a husband.
Me: Thanks for the advice. I'll get right on that.

Honestly, I love the way kids' minds work. They don't necessarily always factor in logistics or reality—they simply believe that essentially anything is possible. I mean, take a boy we'll call Bryce, for instance. When I asked the kindergarteners and first graders what they wanted to be when they grow up, he said that he wanted to be a "donut seller" and charge $20 per donut so that he can be rich. That's ambition. That's hope. That's a dream. Granted, it's not practical, and his likelihood of success with that price isn't great, but he didn't care. Right then, to him, anything was possible, regardless of any outside factors.

What happens as we get older that makes us think that our dreams are less likely to happen for us and to us? What is it that kids have that we don't that allows them to let their hopes soar so high that they're those high-in-the-sky-apple-pie hopes? Why do we lose that childlike faith as our age numbers tick up a notch each year?

Here's the thing: *We don't have to lose that kind of faith.*

I haven't accomplished all of the things in life that I've set out to accomplish. There are some goals I have that are floating out there that I still want so badly to become part of my story. For whatever reason, though, they aren't yet. But that doesn't mean that they never will be, and the lack of them certainly doesn't change my value or sufficiency.

For Bryce and Avery and so many more of those kids, it's simple—you want something, and you're going to make it happen. There are no doubts. There are no fears. There are no hesitations. There are no questions or anxieties or discouragements or logistics or factors or anything that we eventually start to use as determinations of whether or not the desires we have are practical enough or not.

For those believing kids, nothing matters but the fact that they know that the hopes in their hearts are possible, and that's that.

It's not too late to make your dreams realities. It's not too late to set new goals. It's not too late to become the person you've always wanted to be. If you want to be like Bryce and be a donut seller and charge an outrageous amount of money per donut, you do you (and good luck to you).

Your story is just that—*yours*. You aren't required to justify or make excuses or apologies to anyone else for being the person you are. So be you. Go after the desires of your heart. Love people in big ways without caring about what you'll get in return.

And be brave enough never to let go of that childlike faith that once let you live more boldly than you ever knew you could and made you believe that you are enough just as you are.

～ ～

There's one innocent aspect of our childhoods, though, that perhaps we should let fade so that it doesn't end up causing us pain later in life: making wishes.

I went to see *Wicked* in Hollywood with my good friend Amanda and her mom one night shortly before 2018 drew to a close. It was such an amazing performance and overall great play, and the lead roles had incredible voices that I like to pretend I have when I'm singing in the car or the shower. There was a concept from one of the songs that really hit me and got me thinking, though.

Wishing only wounds the heart.

As a girl so full of hopes and dreams that I actually believe are possible, it pierced my heart to hear the words. The more I thought about it, though, the more I realized that wishing truly can wound the heart—a reality that Disney never taught me long ago.

I think that wishing is a lot different than hoping and dreaming. When you have hope, you back it with faith and trust. There's an anticipation, and you let your confident expectation drown out doubt. You have an optimistic outlook, and you might even put some patient endurance behind that positivity. And a dream is a vision you have of something wonderful that doesn't exist yet but will in the future. You work toward it—you strive with everything you have to make that dream come true. There's a need for perseverance and faith as you continue through your journey to get that desired outcome.

A wish, on the other hand, is a longing that you toss out into the air (often silently), and you don't necessarily do anything about it. Why is it that when you make a wish on birthday candles or after you get the bigger end of the wishbone, you aren't allowed to tell anyone what you wished if you actually want it to come true? You can tell people your dreams, and they can support you as you chase them down. You can tell people your hopes, and they can pray for you and alongside you as your hopeful expectations begin to grow.

But wishes are different.

I've made a lot of wishes in my life, and I frequently used to find myself wishing each time I witnessed a shooting star, saw 11:11 on the clock, and got my hands on dandelions. Maybe that's because it's sometimes fun to take part in childlike activities like that—the innocence of it all reminds you of how simple life was before you knew all of the things you wish you didn't. If I'm being perfectly honest, though, a lot of the wishes I made back then were for realities that I didn't always believe in my heart were going to happen.

Which, like the song says, *only wounds the heart.*

Hope deferred makes the heart sick because you believe so positively that what you desire will happen. The actual hoping part itself doesn't hurt—it fills the heart with joy and excitement. But wishing only wounds the heart because there isn't always much confidence behind a wish.

I don't want to be a wisher. I want to be a dreamer and a hoper. I want to go after the dreams I have and fully trust in what the future holds and Who holds it regarding the hopes in my heart. I know that's not always easy, but there are quite a few things in this world that I've faced that have been more challenging, and I've lived through them. I just have to remind myself that I CAN DO HARD THINGS.

In the less than two years that I lived in California, God did a lot of work in my heart and grew my faith in more ways that I ever knew was possible. Moving out there and knowing zero people made it much more apparent to me just how sufficient He is—how He truly is all we need in life. At the same time, though, He surrounded me with amazing people and a tremendous amount of love. That's not something I ever wished for, but it's certainly something that I hoped for with all of my heart.

Shortly after seeing the play, I changed my wishing tactics so that the things I wish don't just stay wishes but, instead, become hopes and dreams. I've spent too many years letting wishing wound my heart, and a heart wasn't made to hurt so much. It wasn't made to break when you're reminded of what you don't have. It wasn't made to ache each time the dandelion particles flying through the air as a result of your breath scatter in every direction. It was made to be brave and to love and love well.

My sweet friend, please don't let wishing diminish your hope—wishing may wound the heart, but hope will fill it with love.

And one hope of mine is that I will take advantage of the surprising memories I encounter before they become memories. I hope you will, too. So many of the days of all of our lives are filled with unexpected moments—some good and others not so great. When the opportunity for an adventure that you weren't anticipating arrives, though, I highly suggest that you take it.

Especially if it involves being surrounding by a bunch of onlookers on a wharf as you reel in a bat ray with a stranger's fishing pole.

Not too long after I had been in California, my friend Ashley and I planned on taking a day road trip before she and her husband moved to Nebraska (I STILL DO NOT WANT TO TALK ABOUT IT). We had originally talked about going to a castle tour and then to some of the areas nearby it, but when I woke up that Saturday morning, a four-hour (or longer) drive didn't seem like the most fun idea—it was far too gorgeous out to be in a car that long. For some reason, while I was running that morning, I thought that Santa Barbara sounded like a much better place to go for an adventure.

When she picked me up for our drive, I ran my idea by her, and she seemed relieved. It turns out that she had also been thinking that we should nix the castle thing, so we agreed that making the shorter trek up to Santa Barbara was the way to go.

If you've never been to Santa Barbara, you should consider changing that. It's truly beautiful and has plenty of quaint areas that make you feel like you're right at home. As soon as we got there, we got food (because, well, priorities), and then we hopped on the trolley with the driver named Jim to take us down to the wharf. I had never been on a wharf, but it was fascinating. We took some pics and then walked to the end and sat to relax and stare out at the water. After a few minutes, we heard a commotion behind us, so we walked over to see what all of the fuss was.

One of the guys fishing had apparently gotten a hold of something big, but whatever it was wasn't going down without a fight. Some people speculated that it was a thresher shark, and the fisherman began walking along the edge of the pier to follow the huge creature's path. Ashley wandered off to go take pictures of seagulls and whatnot, but I was too intrigued to leave the scene. I followed him with my phone because I had started taking videos of the whole spectacle—you never know when something really exciting might happen—and the rather large crowd that had formed started following, as well. The fisherman finally saw that it was a bat ray, handed the pole to his friend, and went to get a net for when he reeled it in. The friend then turned to me, and the following conversation ensued.

Enthusiastic guy: "You wanna fight it?"
Me (thinking he was joking around): "Absolutely, I do."
EG: "You really want to fight it?"
Me (realizing I had never "fought" marine wildlife and thinking maybe "fight" didn't mean an actual fight): "Are you serious?"
EG: "Yeah! Come on, little woman!"
Me: "Little woman? Give me that pole."

The next few moments of my life were ridiculous and awesome all at once. I had told that guy that my name is Natalie and that he needed to stop calling me names that are synonyms for "small." He then kept yelling "Come on, Natalie! Yeah, Nat! Woohoohoo!" I kept reeling and reeling, and I finally got that thing above the water. Fisherman Perry rushed over with a huge net and got the ray inside of it when I reeled it high enough. It took a couple of minutes, but everyone in the crowd watched as he took the hook out of the bat ray and untangled the little fella from the net before tossing him back in the water. He and his pal then gave me public recognition in front of all of those gathered in the area, and I'm sure I bowed or flexed my muscles or something.

And I can now say that I've received applause from a crowd on a wharf for my brute strength.

That unforgettable Saturday turned out to be a day I never

expected, but it was just what I needed. I honestly had no idea what I was doing reeling in that bat ray, and I'm pretty sure that was obvious when I was holding the pole upside down at first and trying to reel the wrong way. I don't fish often (or ever), and I was fairly certain that, with my luck, I was somehow going to fall off of that dock because there weren't any bars or barriers to stop a person from going overboard—and, let's be honest, my track record doesn't exactly exude balance and poise.

The whole experience was different, and it was exciting.

Life doesn't always go the way we think or plan it will. If it did, I would have been watching the Winter Olympics every night that month with the man I love instead of by myself with a bag of candy. I love the quote "when something goes wrong in your life, just yell 'PLOT TWIST,' and move on" (my friend Nona sent this one to me—the Internet tells me Molly Weis said it, and the Internet clearly never lies) because it reminds me to adapt to the unexpected things that come my way instead of being afraid of them. So, if someone hands you a fishing pole and tells you to reel in some large creature you've never heard of, don't be afraid to give it a try.

You might find that you're capable of more than you thought you were.

Some of those abilities you didn't know you had, though, could potentially lead to mistakes that make you feel like the messiness just keeps piling up in life.

And, instead of having a crowd cheer you on as you create a spectacle on a wharf, you might have a hearty crowd to see one of your huge mishaps happen live.

A few weeks after the Santa Barbara trip, I went to my church's winter camp up at Big Bear Mountain as a leader for one of the girls groups in the high school ministry. It was a few days packed full of fun, craziness, and helping kids learn the importance of loving others. As with most of our activities within the high school ministry, there were a variety of games, some of which involved a solid amount of silliness.

On the first morning we were there, we received a full rundown of some rules that were specific to the venue that hosted us for the weekend. One of those rules was not to pull the fire alarms unless there was an actual fire emergency. We were all warned about the trouble and fine by the fire department that would ensue if an alarm were pulled when there weren't any actual flames or smoke. The guy in charge also told us that, because we knew all of this and because there wouldn't be any planned fire drills that weekend, any alarm meant that there was a real fire, and we all needed to evacuate and head to a specified location of safety that he mentioned.

Almost immediately after that reminder speech, we went to our meeting space for a few games and a message for the high schoolers (there were also students in the fourth and fifth grades as well as students in junior high at the camp). We played a game called "Poser"—as soon as a pose popped up on the screen, you had to mimic it. The judges chose the worst poser each time, and that person was out. I was right next to an exit door, so when the handstand pose was shown, I decided to use that to help keep me balanced. Here's the prob: There was a fire alarm right next to the door, and I definitely hadn't noticed it.

I think you know where this is going.

Somehow—a way that I will never truly know—my foot managed to hit the alarm and pull it completely down. I honestly didn't really feel it too much, but when I was standing upright, I looked over and saw my co-leader Kate's face with a sheer look of horror and panic on it. I was wondering what she was worried about because I thought maybe I had accidentally opened the door somehow, but I didn't think that was such a bad thing.

Then a piercing and persistent noise began that let me know that I had done something much worse.

The moments that followed were filled with chaos, people making jokes to me about my little slip-up, and others trying to assure me that it was just an accident and that surely I wouldn't have to pay the massive fine to the fire department. I already started mentally preparing for that fine and thinking of how I could convince them to let me get on a monthly payment plan.

One of the other leaders had sprinted down to the main office of the camp (in the cold and misty rain, mind you) to let the head honcho know that it was a false alarm and to see if he could please call the fire department so that it wouldn't send a truck full of good-looking firemen out. Even though we didn't get to see the eye candy, it was actually a much better situation for me, because it meant that I didn't have to pay the enormous amount of moolah to cover the fine.

I'm not going to lie—I do a lot of clumsy things in my life, but this one affected more than just me. I mean, all of the elementary and junior high kids had already started evacuating their buildings, and some of those poor students probably thought it was a real fire, which likely spooked some of the younger ones quite a bit. And that wasn't the only thing I did that pointed out my flaws that weekend—I also spilled a bunch of batteries everywhere when I was trying to turn off an electric candle, spilled Cinnamon Toast Crunch all over the cabin room floor when I was trying to clean up, got lost on a morning run in an area that I didn't know (and ended up having to hop a fence because of it), and took my girls into the closed dining hall to get some tea to take back to our rooms (but, as it turns out, we were not allowed to be in there at the time). It's also possible that I stole a book that I thought belonged to our student ministries leader but didn't. To the former owner of that book, I AM SORRY FOR MY THEFT.

But all of my flaws and all of my failures are part of who I am.

I know I'm not perfect, and I'm very aware that I never will be. Sometimes I try to be, but I'm way too human for that to be possible. One thing I try to focus more on is loving others well. I want people to know that they are valued, that they are loved, and that they matter and that nothing can change that—including the things they do that make them feel ashamed or possibly even stupid.

I've also been trying to love myself better in spite of my failures, as well. How can I expect those I love to believe what I'm telling them and live lives that reflect it if I can't even do so myself? It took years, but I've gotten to a point at which I can kick fire alarms and accidentally break rules without beating myself up about it. I used to think that some of the things that made me me—like my quirks and klutziness and lack of heart-stealing beauty—made me not good enough for guys to love me. But what I have to remind myself of often and what I continue to remind women of all walks of life is that it doesn't matter what guys (or anyone else, for that matter) think of us, because God made us as we are to be the people we're supposed to be.

I guarantee that I'm going to mess up many more times in life. I mean, I'll probably make multiple mistakes today alone. It is another day, after all. But mistakes often lead to lessons, and lessons often lead to growth. We won't always know why they happen to us or because of us, but those mistakes and those failures and those moments when you want to crawl in holes and hide for a while are all integral parts of our stories. I think that getting knocked down and getting back up again (you know, like Chumbawamba, though I'm pretty sure that the subject matter isn't the same here) is bold. It takes courage, and it takes accepting and admitting that you aren't as perfect as you'd like to be—and that's OK.

Even if you end up kick a fire alarm or two along the way.

24

Because Anything Matches If You Wear It with Confidence

After more than a year of living in California, I was feeling much more comfortable and settled in—but never quite at home. There was something about it that always still felt foreign and temporary. I tried to tell myself that it was simply because I had access to the beach whenever I wanted, but it was more than that. It wasn't my home, and I knew it. The only thing I didn't know was how long I would be there trying to make it feel like more of a home.

Right around Thanksgiving in the fall of 2018, I started to become a bit homesick. The same thing had happened the year before, so I wasn't too concerned about it and wrote it off as me coming down with a little trace of the holiday blues. I went home to Texas for Thanksgiving, and my feelings continued to grow as I returned to California. I had just spent a few days soaking up every precious moment I could with my people, and it felt right.

I started praying more adamantly about these feelings I was having, asking God to take them away or to let me know what they meant. I needed clarity and direction and wisdom and discernment.

On a Sunday evening in early December, three of the girls I led in the high school group at church made the decision to be baptized, and I was the one who had the honor to baptize them. It was by far one of the most special moments of my life to be there for them and walk alongside them as they made this decision. I had seen them all grow so much over that past year, and I loved witnessing how much the Lord had changed their hearts in such a short amount of time.

As I was leaving church that evening, I remember praying and asking God, "See, how can I walk away from this, Lord?" But then I heard His voice again.

You're not going to be with them forever. I am.

Another sucker punch of truth. Those girls didn't need me in their lives—He's all they needed and all they will ever need every single day of their lives. Sure, they would be sad if I left, and I would be equally as upset, but we didn't actually need each other. People can't complete people, no matter what Jerry Maguire says.

The next morning, I was at my desk at work and letting too many anxieties fill my mind: *What am I supposed to do? I love California. Why would I leave after finally finding community with people and being able to step in to some leadership roles at church? I like being plugged in. But I miss Dallas and my people. I don't feel at home here. Why don't I know what to do? I hate decisions.*

So I did the only thing that ever makes sense to me in moments like that: I prayed. *God, when You called me out here, You made it completely clear to me that it was what I was supposed to do. I need that again. You know I need that. Please give me clarity on whether I'm meant to stay here or go back to Dallas.*

Not two hours later, I was reading *Uninvited* by Lysa TerKeurst (a book I highly recommend, by the way) at lunch, when everything became so entirely real and true, and all of the haze and confusion from the past few weeks disappeared. There's a part in the book when Lysa is trying to talk herself into jumping from a pole in one of those obstacle things in which you're harnessed in and attempting to grab a bar hanging in the air after your leap. Her feet weren't moving, so her friend Bob Goff (another author I advise you to check out) came alongside her and finally said the thing that gave her the courage she had been trying to find all along: "You're absolutely loved. Whenever you're ready, jump."

As soon as I read that line, I once again heard that voice that has guided me and comforted me through so much already: *There's your answer, my sweet girl. It's time.*

In that instant on Monday, December 4, 2018, I knew that I was going home soon—and I couldn't help but smile and feel more than a bit relieved. I had asked Cristy to pray about it for me earlier that morning, and after I texted my sister that I was moving home, I immediately called Cristy and relayed everything that had just happened. We celebrated together, and my heart was filled with even more joy after talking everything through with her.

THANK YOU, JESUS. I'M GOING HOME.

If I'm being perfectly honest, though, there was a little bit of fear inside of me. It wasn't fear about having to start over yet again or leaving behind some pretty incredible people and a beautiful place of sunshine and beach days. Rather, it was a fear of failure. *Did moving home mean that I wasn't capable of living in a world of the unknown all by myself? Had I let myself down? Was it childish and wimpy to move home just because I missed my people and my place?*

But then I had to stop. And breathe. And thank God again. And trust Him. I hadn't failed. I had done the hard thing, and I had lived through it. I had enjoyed it. I had grown and learned and gained community and healed and led others and become humbled and discovered truths I had never known.

Even though there were moments filled with doubts and tears and frustrations galore, I will always be thankful for the time I had in California, and I wouldn't trade the time that I was out there for anything. It was what I needed during that season of my life, and I was able to make some wonderful memories and lasting friendships in the process.

We all have different paths and journeys we take in life, and they won't all look the same. They shouldn't. At the end of the *Wizard of Oz*, Dorothy said that she wouldn't ever again go searching for the desires of her heart outside of the confines of her backyard, because those desires wouldn't be found anywhere else. I don't completely agree with that, though. I think that sometimes you have to allow yourself to step outside of your comfort zone to learn and grow and become the person you were always meant to be. It might lead you right back to your backyard, but at least you stepped out to somewhere new and allowed yourself to be braver than you thought you could be. (Dorothy was right about the "no place like home" thing, though.)

If other people wouldn't be surprised that I was moving home and had predicted it all along, so be it. I'm not their opinions of me. I had been brave, and I started to feel like moving back to Texas was also a brave thing to do. It's OK to give yourself little pep talks every now and again, my friend. I'm often really good at offering encouragement to others but then not so great about giving myself the same levels of affirmation. That needed to change in this situation, and I made sure to remind myself that I was doing the right thing. I knew with all of my heart that I was, and I was incredibly excited about it; there was no need to squelch all of that joy with lies and feelings of inadequacy.

I learned more than I ever knew about the lies we tell ourselves while I was out there. I had thought I was a huge advocate of feminism and reminding people that they're enough, but those passions began stirring in my heart in enormous increments while I was living on the West Coast. I can't explain exactly why it didn't happen until then, although I think it was mainly because I was on my own and relying solely on the Lord (which is how I should always be living my life, regardless of my circumstances), and He reminded me more and more of His sufficiency and my identity in Him. More than ever, I wanted (and still want) everyone to feel like they matter. Like they're loved. Like they're valued. Like they're enough.

And I want them to believe every single word of that truth.

We live in a highly imperfect world, and it's going to let us down more than we can ever expect. That's why we need to be lights and love to others, even when they aren't to us. And that's why we need to make sure that we show ourselves love, as well.

People might ridicule you or judge you or make you feel like there's something about you that makes you inadequate. It's also possible that you will or already do believe those lies about yourself without the help of anyone else making you think them. Stop believing those lies, and start reminding yourself that you are worth the investment in yourself to believe that you are capable and worthy of what your heart desires.

Lies are destructive, so remind yourself of this truth: *You are enough.* And please believe it.

You were created on purpose. You're not here by accident, and you're going through the things you're going through for some reason that you may not know now or even ever. But I encourage you to trust where you are and to trust Whose you are. He won't ever let you down, and I fully know that with every ounce of my being and every beat of my mending heart.

I hope that you believe that it's good to be you. Stop comparing yourself to everyone else, and start living each day with the confidence that you are enough and that you are beautiful and worthy as you are. Don't let other people form your opinions of yourself or how you should live your life. It's not theirs to live. They can't change who you are if you don't let them. You aren't defined by your hobbies or status or by people or their opinions.

Being brave as you follow the passions in your heart and knowing each step of the way that your identity isn't found in people or things helps you to become more and more comfortable being you and doing the things that you know you're supposed to do and the things that your heart is calling you to do.

Which is why *anything matches if you wear it with confidence.*

Acknowledgements

As I sat down to write this, I wanted to say thank you to every single human I've ever met, because I'm sure that each interaction has had an impact on me in one way or another. But I also want to make sure to acknowledge specific individuals who have meant more to me than they might know. You are my people, and I love y'all.

To Jesus, my everything. You love me when I don't deserve love. You give me grace when I don't deserve grace. You are all I need.

To my sister, thank you for being you. You're the most beautiful person I know—inside and out—and I love you forever and always. Don't ever lose that light in your eyes.

To my mom and dad, thank you for supporting me in all that I do. You've always encouraged me to follow my dreams, and that's helped me to take chances that I never knew I could. Together, you two are a beautiful example of what lifelong love looks like, and I'm more than grateful for you both.

To my nieces, thank you for being my little besties. You made me an aunt, and it's a love that fills me with more joy than I knew could exist. And thank you, Chris, for knowing how much they mean to me and making sure that I'm able to spend time with them.

To my sweet cousin Rachel, thank you for always making time for me and reminding me of who I am in Him. You're more than a blessing, and I adore you.

To my Aunt Vickie and Uncle Bobcat, I love y'all more than

words can say, and I cherish each moment with y'all. Thank you for your constant love and support.

To my precious friend and mentor Cristy, thank you for being my go-to prayer warrior and an incredible role model. You radiate more joy and love than anyone I know, and I'm always grateful for our early morning Starbucks chats.

To one of my favorite California blessings, sweet Ashley English, thank you for being an incredible friend who knows what it means to be genuine and caring at all times. And thank you for proofing this book. You have a heart of love, and I'm forever grateful for you.

To my forever friend Mads, thank you for your encouragement and for being my own personal professional photographer. You're a true gem.

To Kimbo and Prez, thank you for your beautiful hearts, constant laughter, and ability to make people smile every single day.

To Amanda and Val, thank you for always reminding me of what true friendship looks like. VAN forever.

To my gratitude gems, thank you for keeping our weekly tradition alive. I love y'all with my whole heart.

To Jaderade, Fritzy, Talena, Piper, Anna J, and Mel, thank you for being walking hearts who are always there for me and always rooting for me. You are treasures for sure.

To my students, thank you for being the unique individuals you are—yes, all of you.

To Dallas and Orange County, thank you for being beautiful places that have served as homes for me and allowed me to meet some of the most remarkable people I'll ever know.

To all of the boys who broke my heart, thank you for teaching me some valuable life lessons that helped me to become a stronger individual.

Printed in the United States
By Bookmasters